AN

INTRODUCTION

to CHRISTIAN

MYSTICISM

Recovering the Wildness
of Spiritual Life

Jason M. Baxter

Baker Academic

a division of Baker Publishing Group
Grand Rapids, Michigan

© 2021 by Jason M. Baxter

Published by Baker Academic
a division of Baker Publishing Group
PO Box 6287, Grand Rapids, MI 49516-6287
www.bakeracademic.com

Printed in the United States of America

Library of Congress Cataloging-in-Publication Control Number: 2020051910

ISBN 978-1-5409-6122-8 (paper)
ISBN 978-1-5409-6439-7 (casebound)

21 22 23 24 25 26 27   7 6 5 4 3 2 1

In keeping with biblical principles of creation stewardship, Baker Publishing Group advocates the responsible use of our natural resources. As a member of the Green Press Initiative, our company uses recycled paper when possible. The text paper of this book is composed in part of post-consumer waste.

Contents

Acknowledgments

T hanks to my colleague Kyle Washut for answering all my questions about Neoplatonic ontology. He made me wish that there was a hotline for burning questions about Byzantine metaphysics. I thank my friends Glenn and Virginia Arbery for their unflagging encouragement. Special thanks to Colum Dever, who reminded me that Jesus, the God who became a helpless baby, needs to feature in any discussion of Christian mysticism. The conclusion is for you. And warm thanks to my editor, Dave Nelson, whose energy and kindness drew out my best.

I'd like to thank my wonderful students for listening to drafts of the chapters that follow and responding with such overwhelming goodness, especially Cami Callaway, Louisa Whitmore, Emily Mistaleski, Ana and Sophie Kozinski, Rinju Chenet, Tommy Urgo, Zach Lee, Parker Eidle, Anna Snell, Rocco De Felice, Evelyn Grimm, Brendan Floody, Carlos Solis, Eastlyn Ullman, Joseph Maxwell, and Iza Zagorksi.

I dedicate this book to my beloved wife and children: Jodi, Pia, Eve-Marie, John-Marie, Alma, and Jude. With more love than you could know.

Abbreviations

Conf.	Augustine. *Confessions*. Translated by F. J. Sheed. 2nd ed. Indianapolis: Hackett, 2006.
Ladder	Guigo the Carthusian. *The Ladder of Monks and Twelve Meditations: A Letter on the Contemplative Life*. Translated by Edmund Colledge and James Walsh. Kalamazoo, MI: Cistercian Publications, 1981.
Life	Gregory of Nyssa. *The Life of Moses*. Translated by Abraham J. Malherbe and Everett Ferguson. Classics of Western Spirituality. Mahwah, NJ: Paulist Press, 1980.
LSF	Bonaventure. *The Life of St. Francis*. In *Bonaventure*, translated by Ewert Cousins, 177–328. Classics of Western Spirituality. Mahwah, NJ: Paulist Press, 1978.
Mem.	Angela of Foligno. *Memorial*. In *Angela of Foligno: Complete Works*, translated by Paul Lachance, 123–218. Classics of Western Spirituality. Mahwah, NJ: Paulist Press, 1993.
MT	Pseudo-Dionysius. *Mystical Theology*. In *Pseudo-Dionysius: The Complete Works*, translated by Colm Luibheid, 133–42. Classics of Western Spirituality. Mahwah, NJ: Paulist Press, 1987.
On Loving God	Bernard of Clairvaux. *On Loving God*. In *Bernard of Clairvaux: Selected Works*, translated by G. R. Evans, 173–206. Classics of Western Spirituality. Mahwah, NJ: Paulist Press, 1987.
On Seeking God	Nicholas of Cusa. *On Seeking God*. In *Nicholas of Cusa: Selected Spiritual Writings*, translated by H. Lawrence

	Bond, 215–32. Classics of Western Spirituality. Mahwah, NJ: Paulist Press, 1997.

On the Vices   Evagrius. *To Eulogios: On the Vices as Opposed to the Virtues.* In *Evagrius of Pontus: The Greek Ascetic Corpus*, translated by Robert E. Sinkewicz, 60–65. Oxford: Oxford University Press, 2003.

Praktikos   Evagrius. *The Monk: A Treatise on the Practical Life.* In *Evagrius of Pontus: The Greek Ascetic Corpus*, translated by Robert E. Sinkewicz, 91–114. Oxford: Oxford University Press, 2006.

Rule   Benedict. *RB 1980: The Rule of St. Benedict in English.* Edited and translated by Timothy Fry. Collegeville, MN: Liturgical Press, 1981.

Sayings   *The Sayings of the Desert Fathers: The Alphabetical Collection.* Translated by Benedicta Ward. New York: Macmillan, 1975.

Sermon 12   Meister Eckhart. Sermon 12. In *Meister Eckhart: Selected Writings*, translated by Oliver Davies, 152–58. London: Penguin, 1994.

Showings   Julian of Norwich. *Julian of Norwich: Showings.* Translated by Edmund Colledge and James Walsh. Classics of Western Spirituality. Mahwah, NJ: Paulist Press, 1978.

Sparkling Stone   John Ruusbroec. *The Sparkling Stone.* In *John Ruusbroec: "The Spiritual Espousals" and Other Works*, translated by James Wiseman, 155–86. Classics of Western Spirituality. Mahwah, NJ: Paulist Press, 1985.

Three Days   Hugh of St. Victor. *On the Three Days.* In *Trinity and Creation*, translated by Hugh Feiss, 49–102. Victorine Texts in Translation 1. Edited by Boyd Taylor Coolman and Dale M. Coulter. New York: New City Press, 2011.

Zion   Hugh of Balma. *The Roads to Zion Mourn.* In *Carthusian Spirituality: The Writings of Hugh of Balma and Guigo de Ponte*, translated by Dennis Martin, 67–170. Classics of Western Spirituality. Mahwah, NJ: Paulist Press, 1997.

Introduction

The Soul from Whom God Hides Nothing

I pray we could come to this darkness so far above light! If only we lacked sight and knowledge so as to see, so as to know, unseeing and unknowing, that which lies beyond all vision and knowledge.

—Pseudo-Dionysius the Areopagite, *Mystical Theology*

A Quick Sketch of Mysticism

Over the past few years, when teaching Dante to college students, I've found it necessary to provide a quick outline of mysticism by way of background to Dante's final canticle, *Paradiso*. I've noticed, though, that as I talk about ineffability and the Platonic tradition of a "God beyond being" and the necessity of waking up a "sense" that is above reason, my students are overcome by a sense of trepidation. On more than one occasion, noticing that my students have stiffened up and have begun to look at me suspiciously, I've paused to ask, "Is this stuff making you nervous?" The answer is usually yes, because it seems to them somehow vaguely "Eastern" or associated with New Age spirituality.

Take, for example, Meister Eckhart, the fourteenth-century German Dominican who, along with the sixth-century Byzantine

1

Dionysius the Areopagite (also known as Pseudo-Dionysius), is often thought of as "the mystic's mystic." Eckhart was a celebrity professor in his day, a sometime provost at the University of Paris, and a biblical commentator who also undertook the difficult task of preaching in the vernacular (in his case, German). Here's what he says in one of his German-language sermons:

> In created things, as I have often said before, there is no truth. But there is something which is above the created being of the soul and which is untouched by any createdness, by any nothingness. Even the angels do not have this, whose clear being is pure and deep. . . . It is like the divine nature; in itself it is one and has nothing in common with anything. And it is with regard to this that many teachers go wrong. It is a strange land, a wilderness, being more nameless than with name, more unknown than known. If you could do away with yourself for a moment, even for less than a moment, then you would possess all that this possesses in itself. But as long as you have any regard for yourself in any way or for anything, then you will not know what God is. As my mouth knows what colour is and my eye what taste is: that is how little you will know what God is.[1]

These words are as frightening as they are intriguing. Eckhart says that we know as much about God as the eye knows about tasting or the tongue tells us about color, because we've been using the wrong faculty to experience him. God is above our reason, above our consciousness, and even above our morality. He dwells in a special "uncreated" part of the soul, and to move into that part of the soul requires "doing away with yourself." It is like venturing into a nameless desert, an unknown wilderness, a strange land.

I'm sympathetic to the reaction of my students and the other audiences I address because I know they want to be faithful Christians and are afraid of adulterating the message of Christ. But the more I've read, the more I've been struck by the fact that, in the premodern age (that is, what is now called late antiquity and the Middle Ages—everything, you could say, before AD 1500), "mysticism" wasn't some bizarre, exotic, cultish, or unusual phenomenon (like it has become), stored on bookshelves dealing with paranormal occurrences; rather, it was seen as the lifeblood of prayer and adoration of God in the soul. For this reason, it's too precious to stay silent on. Ignoring it would be like selling a precious family heirloom at an estate sale because you didn't know what it was.

Some of my readers might be nervous about mysticism not because they associate it with Eastern religions (Hinduism, Buddhism, or Sufism) but because it feels to them like a "Catholic" or "Orthodox" thing, assuming that it is not for them. George Eliot, though no Protestant, voiced this assumption of nineteenth-century Protestant England in her characterization of the quaint but enticing Mediterranean spirituality of Teresa of Ávila at the beginning of her novel *Middlemarch*.[2] Similarly, I remember reading as a teenager the stern warning of Presbyterian theologian B. B. Warfield, whose words made me suspicious of mysticism for a decade: "The common element in all these varieties of mysticism is that they all seek . . . the knowledge of God in human feelings, which they look upon as the sole or at least the most trustworthy or the most direct source of the knowledge of God."[3] In light of this, Warfield adds, we should be wary of mysticism because Christianity ought to be founded on reason and external authority. Even C. S. Lewis, who corresponded with the greatest scholar of mysticism of his day, Evelyn Underhill, and whose academic background made him interested in medieval spirituality, cautioned against "indulging" in it too much. In his sermon "The Weight of Glory," for example, after soaring to some incredible heights of theological speculation, he reins himself in and warns people about getting carried away:

> What would it be to taste at the fountain-head that stream of which even these lower reaches prove so intoxicating? Yet that, I believe, is what lies before us. The whole man is to drink joy from the fountain of joy. As St. Augustine said, the rapture of the

saved soul will "flow over" into the glorified body. In the light of
our present specialized and depraved appetites we cannot imagine
this *torrens voluptatis*, and I warn everyone seriously not to try.[4]

As a final example, at the beginning of the twentieth century
the incredibly influential Protestant theologian Adolf von Harnack worried about "Hellenic" interpolations into an original,
pure Christianity. If Luther distrusted medieval Scholasticism, von
Harnack pushed his own doubts back to an even earlier stage:
the encroachment of Greek philosophy into the primitive church.
According to von Harnack, we should be on our guard against all
"Greek" ideas, which form the backbone of the medieval Christian
articulation of mysticism.[5]

I will not be able to convince all my readers that mysticism is
a fundamental part of Christianity—Protestant, Orthodox, and
Catholic. However, I would like to make it easier for some of my
readers to be patient with it, to listen to it, to give credence to it.
And so, in this book, I'll focus on writings from before the Protestant Reformation and Catholic Counter-Reformation. Writings
subsequent to that time often feel the pressure to reject things
because they're Catholic, or to double down on things because
they're *not* Protestant. Although I will occasionally refer to post-
Reformation figures to illustrate some particular point, I want to
focus on a time when Christianity was (nominally at least) united.
Even in those writings from after the Great Schism between the
Eastern and Western churches (1054), we'll be able to see that
their authors were still drawing from a shared store of texts and
ideas, hopes and ambitions.

It is true that, without the Greek philosophical tradition, we
would not have the texts and ideas that I will discuss below. Without Plotinus, there would be no Augustinian flight of the soul (as
described in *Confessions* 7, 9, and 10). Without Proclus, there
would be no Dionysius the Areopagite. Without Dionysius and
Augustine, there would be no Eckhart or Cusanus. The Platonic
tradition in particular (see chap. 2) provided early Christians

with the terminology, methodology, and impulse to describe and classify the experience of God systematically—in other words, it provided the skeleton of what has come to be known as *mystical theology*. And this goes straight to the heart of the paradox of Western writings in the Christian mystical tradition: although they are concerned with experiences of God that are beyond language and rationality, almost every mystical treatise is preoccupied with demarcating the steps, grading the stages, outlining the method, and describing the overall system in which such experiences play out. Medieval authors love artificial schema and visual aids to help them hold it all together: steps on a ladder, wings on a seraphim, rooms in the ark, chambers in a castle, and so on. Perhaps pre-modern writers on mysticism are so cautious, so concerned with classifying the steps and describing the preliminary preparation for the mystical journey, because it is easy to confuse a subjective emotional high, or a sincere desire to go deep, with the experience of depth itself. In any case, this is, I think, the biggest surprise for modern readers. If you are mainly accustomed to reading modern spiritual authors, who like to anthologize and talk about only the most sublime and rapturous moments from ancient texts, and *then* you turn to the old authors themselves, you'll be surprised by how much space they devote to nonmystical matters. The paradox is that mystical writers spend a great deal of time discussing the rational intellect, or virtue, or pious practices. And if you come with the wrong expectations, you'll be disappointed when you find that about 89 percent of these treatises have nothing to do with "the good stuff," the sublime encounter with God. This emphasis on the rational and foundational elements in Christian mysticism is an inheritance of the Greek (and Roman) philosophical tradition.

But this does not mean that Christian mysticism is only a "Greek thing" pure and simple. If mysticism is, at its core, a desire to be someone "from whom God hides nothing" (to paraphrase Meister Eckhart)[6]—that is, to know the fullness of God in the depths of one's soul—then we find it anticipated, already everywhere, within the Scriptures. For example, when God calls out to the burning bush ("Moses, Moses. . . . Draw not nigh off thy shoes from off thy feet"), Moses understand-.es] his face; for he was afraid to look upon God" (Exod. 3:4–6,. .ater, on Mount Sinai, the Lord tells Moses that "it is a terrible thing that I will do with thee" (34:10), and when the Lord descends "in the cloud," Moses, again overcome by the awe-filled presence of God, "made haste, and bowed his head toward the earth, and worshipped" (34:8). Elsewhere, we read that Moses conceived the audacious desire to see the face of God uncovered, and that the Lord spoke to him "face to face, as a man speaketh unto his friend" (33:11).

We also read in the Old Testament that Isaiah saw the Lord "sitting upon a throne, high and lifted up, and his train filled the temple." God was surrounded by seraphim who were crying out, while the "posts of the door moved at the voice of him that cried, and the house was filled with smoke" (Isa. 6:1, 4). Isaiah, too, was terrified: "Then said I, Woe is me! For I am undone; . . . for mine eyes have seen the King, the LORD of hosts" (6:5). Poor Ezekiel, when the word of the Lord came "expressly" unto him (Ezek. 1:3), beheld a vision of a whirlwind out of the north, "a great cloud, and a fire infolding itself, and a brightness was about it," and all kinds of phantasmagorical wheels and creatures and gems: "This was the appearance of the likeness of the glory of the LORD. And when I saw it, I fell upon my face" (1:4, 28). Abraham had a "deep sleep" fall upon him: "And lo, an horror of great darkness fell upon him" (Gen. 15:12). He later entertained angels (Gen. 18), while Jacob had his thigh put out of joint by an angel (Gen. 32:25) and was given a vision of a ladder with angels ascending and descending on it (28:12). When Jacob woke up from his vision of the ladder, he found himself in a cold sweat: "And Jacob awaked out of his sleep, and he said, Surely the LORD is in this place; and I knew it not. And he was afraid, and said, How dreadful is this place! This is none other but the house of God, and this is the gate of heaven" (28:16–17). In scriptural encounters with God, the human beholders are inevitably stupefied, overwhelmed, or overawed by how much the divine beauty, power, and glory exceeds their previous expectations.

In the New Testament we find the same pattern. The disciples briefly see Christ transparent in his glory: as Jesus prays, "the fashion of his countenance was altered, and his raiment was white and glistering" (Luke 9:29). As you might expect, the disciples with Jesus "fell on their face, and were sore afraid" (Matt. 17:6). Meanwhile, Peter babbles nonsense. Paul, who finds himself suddenly enveloped in a bright light from heaven in his encounter with Christ, accordingly "fell to the earth" (Acts 9:4), as does John during his vision on Patmos (Rev. 1:17). And, most mysteriously of all, Paul alludes autobiographically to an ecstatic rapture into heaven: "I knew a man in Christ above fourteen years ago . . . [who] was caught up into paradise, and heard unspeakable words, which it is not lawful for a man to utter" (2 Cor. 12:2–4).

These scriptural narratives are profoundly moving, almost disturbing. The God who made the world cannot be contained within it. If you try to look at God from within the world, so to speak, you're limiting what you can see. But in select moments the screen, the veil, is ripped away, and the human beholders are left gaping, inarticulately, at what's behind.

When early Christian and medieval authors steeped in these scriptural accounts also got access to the best of paganism, an extraordinary thing happened: they tried to frame out the wild and disorienting narratives of Scripture in the articulate and precise terms they found in their beloved pagan authors. For example, Gregory of Nyssa used his Greek learning to map out a path in which we "ordinary" Christians can presume to lead a life like that of Moses. Similarly, Augustine confesses that he longs to see God's face, echoing a sentiment drawn from the life of Moses, but he borrows from the vocabulary of Greek writers like Plotinus. The writer known as Pseudo-Dionysius the Areopagite adopted the literary persona of being Paul's disciple. Schooled in the most sophisticated Athenian Platonism of his day, he claimed that his writings were meant to explicate the vision that Paul cryptically described in 2 Corinthians 12. The combination of these two traditions (Greek and scriptural) created a desire and a strategy to be someone "from whom God hides nothing." In other words, it resulted in mysticism, a kind of holy presumptuousness in which I, an "ordinary" Christian, refuse to accept that great encounters with God are the exclusive privilege of biblical heroes. I begin to desire to see the Lord "sitting upon a throne, high and lifted up," as did Isaiah; to get a glimpse of the fullness of reality that lies behind the veil, as did Ezekiel and John; and to be "the Friend of God," like Abraham was (James 2:23). The mystic believes, along with C. S. Lewis, that in the end, "there are no ordinary people. You have never talked to a mere mortal."[7]

What Is Mysticism?

We're now ready to take our first shot at answering the question, What is mysticism? Maybe it's better to start with what mysticism is *not*. It's not about voices or visions. It's not a whimsical or capricious Shakerism in which you are violently seized with a personal revelation.[8] Rather, it's the fruit of love and virtue and patience and diligence in prayer and discipleship. Mysticism is about God, beauty, prayer, and the depth of the soul. Through the careful development of character and the training of the mind, it aims to achieve an *intellectual* vision—that is, unmediated contact with God. But this intellectual vision is hard to win. Technically, you can't "win" it at all; it's a gift. Nevertheless, to achieve this intellectual vision, to get to the "highest point" of your soul (as Augustine puts it), you have to pass through the prior stages of purgation of the heart and purgation of the mind until the practice of charity (including intellectual charity) becomes natural. In this way, mysticism is a rational, ethical, and systematic preparation for an experience of the fullness of God.

But there's more. Mysticism is founded on the belief that every soul is made with an infinite desire that only an infinite bliss can satisfy.[9] Mysticism believes that this infinite fountain for which our souls thirst is God, but God cannot be contained within the creation he made, nor can he be comprehended fully within human language and rationality, by which we represent that creation in our minds. Thus, mysticism is an ascent through rationality toward the edge of language, and when we have arrived at the periphery of language, we walk over the edge and fall into the "darkness of unknowing," as Dionysius calls it, which is not ignorance but a way of knowing that is higher and deeper than our customary rational consciousness. In other words, mysticism is made up of a "learned ignorance," as Nicholas of Cusa calls it. This darkness of unknowing is a moment of deep connection, of union, of closeness, and of presence.[10] It is fundamentally the Mosaic desire to see God face-to-face; or, as the Cistercian Gilbert of Hoyland thought, it is the real meaning hiding behind Psalm 42:7: "Deep calleth unto deep at the noise of thy waterspouts: all thy waves and thy billows are gone over me." Gilbert reads "abyss calls unto abyss" as the abyss of divine love that calls out from the very depths of our own souls, so that as we turn inward we become immersed in the "measureless ocean of Divine Majesty," the "abyss of hidden light."[11]

At the same time, the mystic, moved within by this holy presumption, realizes that to reach this pinnacle in which the Maker of the world, unveiled, addresses a person, one must pass through a period of discipleship, discipline, and even painful darkness and lonely abnegation. I have to develop a taste for eternity, and so I have to break the addictive craving for temporal things. And then I even have to move beyond my own morality, realizing that being "good" is not good enough. I have to move beyond my expectation that I can "know" God. Because God is the maker of heaven and earth—the world of "being"—he cannot be found within it. Thus, my language and reasoning are inadequate to know him. I have to develop a deeper power of "knowing"—that is, to open the "inner eye" or "interior vision," as the ancient pagan philosopher Plotinus puts it (see below). When I come to the pinnacle of my soul, I have to step out into darkness, leaving even my reason behind. Because this is frightening, it takes epic ambition or, as one scholar puts it, an extraordinary treasury of "intellectual generosity."[12] This daring quest, this soaring ascent "up" to God, leads us into that "unnameable" part of the soul (which is, paradoxically, deeper down within me than I am to myself). And so, in the mystical tradition we have a paradoxical juxtaposition of inwardness and upwardness, a quest that leads me to the core of my personality by way of the highest point of reality.

Because the mystical quest ventures out into a space beyond language and even beyond "knowing," there is an important poetic aspect within the mystical tradition. Indeed, medieval authors frolic in a rich field of metaphors, gathering as many likenesses as they can, all of which at best merely gesture and point to that which is ultimately unsayable. And so, already in these last few paragraphs, I've been speaking of the "barren desert" and retreating into the inner castle of interiority, of soaring and flying up, of deep calling to deep, and of a "cloud of unknowing."[13] Since God is beyond words, mystical writers feel the need to stretch their language to find elaborate and exuberant metaphors for hinting at what is above and below language. In this book we'll hear about the "nudity" of the soul, of falling into a chasm, of plunging into an ocean, of the opening up of an abyss, and, most incredible of all, of the "hurricane" of God's love. In short, all this bold language, which burns like fire and cuts like a sword, is based on the conviction that God is fuller, bigger, and brighter than I can imagine or have ever previously expected. And to "see" or "taste" this, we need to guard ourselves from the tendency to turn God into an idol—to think of him as something small or limited or as some kind of cosmic agent who exists in order to help us be good or get things we want. Mysticism involves setting aside all these idols of the imagination and cravings of the will; it is a resolute purpose to let God be God and a bold entry into the "cloud of unknowing." In the end, mysticism is what happens when God hides nothing from the soul.

Before moving on to the second half of this chapter, I want to pause over a passage from Augustine in which all these themes are present. In his famous description of his ascent at Ostia (*Conf.* IX.10), which I will describe in more detail later, Augustine imagines first ascending the hierarchy of creatures in this world, from caterpillars to supernovas, looking for the most "Godlike" thing in the world. As it turns out, it is not any *thing* but rather the human mind that is the closest "image and likeness" to God. And at the very center of this likeness, there is something that points beyond, to God. Augustine conducts a thought experiment in which the whole world goes silent, and then, he says, we can hear the voice of God from beyond:

> If to any man the tumult of the flesh grew silent, silent the images of the earth and sea and air: and if the heavens grew silent, and the very soul grew silent to herself and by not thinking of self mounted beyond self: if all dreams and imagined visions grew silent, and every tongue and every sign and whatsoever is transient—for indeed if any man could hear them, he should hear them saying with one voice, "We did not make ourselves, but He made us who abides forever": but if, having uttered this and so set us to listening to Him who made them, they all grew silent, and in their silence He alone spoke to us, not by them but by Himself; so that we should hear his word, not by any tongue of flesh nor the voice of an angel nor the sound of thunder nor in the darkness of a parable, but that we should hear Himself whom in all these things we love, should hear Himself and not them. . . . This one [vision] should so ravish and absorb and wrap the beholder in inward joys that his life should eternally be such as that one moment of understanding for which we had been sighing—would this not be: *Enter Thou into the joy of Thy Lord*? (Augustine, *Conf.* IX.10, 179)[14]

The desire to hear God's voice—unmediated—is the fundamental desire of mysticism, and it cannot be confused with some personal commission or specific revelation. The heart hungers for something too "big" for creation to hold. The heart hungers for a vision or a taste or perhaps fragrance of God in the depth of his fullness, and one second of such a moment of encounter is worth more than a lifetime of pious deeds and "correct" opinions: "For a day in thy courts is better than a thousand. I had rather be a doorkeeper in the house of my God, than to dwell in the tents of wickedness" (Ps. 84:10).

If mysticism, rightly understood, is not foreign to Christianity, and if it is, as I have suggested, the lifeblood of the premodern church, then why does it seem so strange and exotic to us? I am convinced that the reason has to do with the fact that we live in a "secular world"—that is, an age in which our fundamental blueprint for thinking about the physical world, our human-ity, and our relationship to God has changed. We might be the weird ones.

How Did We Get Here? Are We the Weird Ones?

Religion has not disappeared from the modern world, of course, but our religious experience and our quest for God unfold now within what philosopher Charles Taylor calls "the immanent frame." By that term he means the social and psychological con-ditions in which God no longer seems as obvious and "palpable" in our world as he did before, say, 1500:

> The presence of something beyond . . . the "natural" is more palpable and immediate, one might say, physical, in an enchanted age. The sacred in the strong sense, which marks out certain people, times, places and actions, in distinction to all others as profane, is by its very nature localizable, and its place is clearly marked out in ritual and sacred geography. This is what we sense, and often regret the passing of, when we contemplate the me-diaeval cathedral. God-forsakenness is an experience of those whose ancestral culture has been transformed and repressed by a relentless process of disenchantment, whose deprivations can still be keenly felt.[15]

The long process of secularization involved a multitude of cultural forces, as Taylor masterfully relates in painstaking detail.
As a result, God and religion are less "obvious" in our cultural
landscape than they used to be; to say it another way, we live in
an age of "practical atheism" or "a-theism."[16] "One way to put
the question . . . is this: why was it virtually impossible not to
believe in God in, say, 1500 in our Western society, while in 2000
many of us find this not only easy, but even inescapable?"[17] This
"every-day" atheism—that is, the recession of the felt presence of
the divine from daily life—is accounted for, in part, by the collapse
of the "bulwarks of belief," those premodern ideas and practices that, though not specifically theological, created a favorable
environment for belief. When everyone believes in an enchanted
cosmos—when the hair on your neck stands up on end when you
leave the boundaries of your parish; when you really worry about
how impish fairies might wish to spellbind your children; when
your court physician, Marsilio Ficino, is an expert in preparing
amulets that you can wear over your heart to help you imbibe
the power of astral bodies—then "religion" does not just make
sense, but indeed the alternative is almost unthinkable. This is the
"porous" world of premodernity, whose heroes are Achilles (who
is hardly surprised to find gods descending to speak to him) and
Roland (who cannot destroy his sword by striking it against a rock
because it has a relic embedded within it). It's a world in which you
cannot escape God; rather, like John Bunyan, you feel his watchful
eye even when you choose to live in a way displeasing to him.[18]

But in contrast to such a premodern, "enchanted" view of the
cosmos—or even to the philosophical visions of Plato and Boethius, who described the cosmos as having a soul that moves
the world, groaning to express something about God[19]—the philosophers of the Scientific Revolution assiduously avoided making any assumptions about the external ends of nature. Nature
must be treated as a "brute creature" and approached as a great
"mechanism," even if it is also true that the scientists of the seventeenth century—they would have called themselves "natural

philosophers"—believed in God and angels and invisible realities, on their own time. Copernicus, Kepler, and Newton were deeply pious, and they thought of themselves as "priests of nature." Robert Boyle even left money in his will to combat atheism! And yet, as it turned out, this habit of approaching the natural world as merely a mechanism (some call it a "methodological naturalism") was, over the slow course of the next centuries, adopted as a *philosophical* paradigm ("philosophical naturalism"). What had been a methodological exclusion of anything but mechanical causes eventually became the assumption that external causes (such as God or spirits) were "merely" religious and thus superfluous for explaining what is really important.[20]

Again, none of this means that, in our secular age, religion has disappeared; rather, it is typically confined to the interior and subjective sphere. Taylor says that whereas we once had a "feeling" that depth of meaning was "out there" somewhere in the universe, we now have transferred that sense onto our interior lives. In Taylor's words, we "conceive of ourselves as having inner depths. We might even say that the depths which were previously located in the cosmos, the enchanted world, are now more readily placed within."[21] In summary, we can borrow Taylor's term "excarnation" to describe the movement from the enchanted world to the disenchanted world: "Official Christianity had gone through what we can call an 'excarnation,' a transfer out of embodied 'enfleshed' forms of religious life, to those which are more 'in the head.'"[22] The result is that we perceive the sacred to have withdrawn from the public sphere and, indeed, from the physical, visible world, so that our ordinary actions can be carried out seemingly without any connection to the sacred.

Louis Dupré's account, like Taylor's, describes the trajectory of secularization from the guarded, whispering, hesitant atheism of a few bold members of the cultural elite in, say, the eighteenth century to the strident "apologetical" atheism of the nineteenth, which in turn yielded to the "benign" atheism that shaped the cultural landscape of everyday life by the beginning of the twentieth.

Significantly, the result of these centuries of slow cultural movement is that our picture of God has changed: how we imagine him, what we feel we need him for. For this reason Dupré argues that Western nihilism actually began in a religious age (!), the age in which God was asked to find his place within our new picture of the world:

> The reduction of the ground of all reality to the sum of separate beings excludes ultimate transcendence. This is exactly what occurs when we refer to God as the supreme *value* or the *cause* of all beings. This abolition of true transcendence is the true atheism of our culture, one which had been developing for centuries before it became manifest and which consists not in the loss of the actual belief in God but in the loss of the very possibility of that belief. In this respect believers even more than unbelievers have failed their God—or in Nietzsche's terms "murdered him"—by lowering him to a scale of being where he can no longer be truly sacred. Thus the concept of God as the supreme value, inclusive of all others, inevitably leads to atheistic rebellion.[23]

In other words, in a world in which materialistic explanations seem sufficient, we often invite God back into the picture, but in a way in which he is imprisoned within that picture of the world. And even when he is invited back (sometimes we don't feel we need him for much), he is expected to hide behind the natural world as its "cause" or "supreme value." In this way, God gets "objectified" and "reified" (reduced to just another thing in the cosmos). Dupré continues:

> When Eckhart refers to God as his very Being, and Ruusbroec as his essence, we are obviously far away from the first cause, the highest value, or the supreme being. For the longest period of its existence our culture remained close to its transcendent source. Only with the advent of the modern era did a fundamental change take place. It appears in such philosophical expressions as "l'auteur de la nature" by which Descartes and his followers refer to God as

a particular piece in the intricate machinery of nature, necessary only because of the need of a cause in a mechanistic universe. Everything of real interest came after the first cause. This would soon enough lead to the bloodless deism of the seventeenth century and, eventually, to the consistent atheistic materialism of the eighteenth and nineteenth centuries.[24]

Changes in our "cosmic imaginary" (our world picture) and metaphysics also have implications for how we think about devotion and morality. In the modern world, God's chief interaction with human beings is to provide a kind of spiritual uplift, a rising tide of morality, the inspiration to be honest, just, disciplined, hardworking, and so on. The scholar Murray Roston contrasts the early seventeenth-century "intensity of belief, the personal fervour," in divines like Lancelot Andrewes and John Donne— where we find a "conviction of the almost desperate condition" of human beings—with what came at the end of that century: a "calmly reasoned advocacy of Christianity as the promoter of ordered and virtuous conduct among rational believers." Whereas Donne plaintively cried out to God to "forgive me my crying sins and my whispering sins, sins of uncharitable hate, and sinnes of unchaste love, sinnes against *Thee* and *Thee*," we find Cambridge theologian and mathematician (and teacher of Newton) Isaac Barrow judiciously arguing that "[Christianity is] a most rational act, arguing the person to be sagacious, considerate, and judicious; one who doth carefully inquire into things, doth seriously weigh the case, doth judge soundly about it." John Tillotson, the archbishop of Canterbury, likewise emphasized a Christianity free from hysterics: "Let us always be calm and considerate, and have the patience to examine things thoroughly and impartially: let us be humble and willing to learn. . . . Let us do what we can to free our selves from prejudice and passion, from self-conceit and self-interest, which are often too strong a bias upon the judgments of the best men."[25] The appeal of such a toned-down approach to religion made sense after several violent centuries of religious divisiveness. "Mysticism," from such a perspective, was dangerous, especially if it was conflated with personal visions, strong emotions, voices from God, and personal commissions. I hardly need to point out that wars, conquests, migrations, and schisms have all been the fruits of such abuses of religion.

And so, in a world in which to be an "enthusiast" or a "zealot" was considered to be dangerously unregulated (see, e.g., David Hume), we can understand the appeal of the kind of piety limiting itself to advancing civic virtues, personal ethics, self-discipline, and tolerance. In such a cultural situation, the main purpose of religion is to promote these virtues. God then becomes a great instrument to supply inspiration and lend a helping hand.

This is, of course, the norm now, as sociologists and journalists point out. What was once a new voice of moderation among the cultural elite has now become the unquestioned background music of our religious lives. We've reached something of a saturation point for this "practical atheism" (or "a-theism"), as was shown in the landmark sociological work by Christian Smith and Melinda Lundquist Denton, *Soul Searching*. Having interviewed three thousand teenagers, they concluded that the religious convictions of modern young people (and the parents who teach them) can be summed up as "moralistic therapeutic deism"—that is, a system of tacit beliefs according to which there is a God who

> exists, created the world, and defines our general moral order, but not one who is particularly personally involved in one's affairs— especially affairs in which one would prefer not to have God involved. Most of the time, the God of this faith keeps a safe distance. He is often described by teens as "watching over everything from above" and "the creator of everything and . . . just up there now controlling everything." . . . For many teens, as with adults, God sometimes does get involved in people's lives, but usually only when they call on him, mostly when they have some trouble or problem or bad feeling that they want resolved. In this sense, the Deism here is revised from its classical eighteenth-century version

by the therapeutic qualifier, making the distant God selectively
available for taking care of needs. . . . This God is not demanding.
He actually can't be, because his job is to solve our problems and
make people feel good.[26]

This quotation appears in a chapter entitled "God, Religion,
Whatever."

Other sociologists and teachers have anecdotally confirmed
Smith and Denton's findings. Kenda Creasy Dean, for example,
argues that the problem is not that American teenagers are getting
the wrong ideas about religion. On the contrary, they're correctly
absorbing what American Christians actually believe! She calls
our general religious view of God the "triumph of the 'cult of
nice.'"[27] Catholic theologian Ulrich Lehner has also commented
on the religious horizons of his students in his book *God Is Not
Nice*: "We have made attending church and believing in God something that nice and polite people do, mostly on Sundays."[28] Lehner
quotes Reinhold Niebuhr, who satirically described the American
religious outlook like this: "A God without wrath brought men
without sin into a Kingdom without judgment through the min-
istrations of a Christ without a Cross."[29] I, too, have had similar
moments in teaching. When I explain moralistic therapeutic deism
to my students, they're always anxious because many of them
recognize it as their own tacit belief system, but they can't envision
what the alternative to a "nice" God and a polite and enthusiastic
religion would look like.

This book is about the alternative.

The Wildness of God: What This Book Is and Is Not

This is not a book about natural theology (an attempt to argue for
the existence of God on the basis of the structure of the world);
nor is it a genealogy of modernity, a history of the Scientific Revolution, or a psychology of religion. Rather, I'm interested in describing the shocking wildness of premodern conceptions of God

and the spiritual life. And so, in the following chapters I will take a series of "core samples" from the premodern mystical tradition, as well as a few modern writers who felt we needed to recover it:

- Plato (who wrote his greatest works in the 370s and 360s BC)
- Plotinus (AD 204–270)
- Gregory of Nyssa (335–395)
- Evagrius (345–399)
- Augustine (354–430)
- John Cassian (360–435)
- Dionysius the Areopagite (early 500s)
- Bernard of Clairvaux (1090–1153)
- Hugh of St. Victor (1096–1141)
- Hildegard of Bingen (1098–1179)
- Guigo II (abbot of Grande Chartreuse, 1174–1180)
- Francis (1181/2–1226)
- Bonaventure (1221–1274)
- Angela of Foligno (1248–1309)
- Meister Eckhart (ca. 1260–1328)
- John Ruusbroec (1293/4–1381)
- Hugh of Balma (probably writing sometime around 1300)
- Julian of Norwich (1342–1416)
- Nicholas of Cusa (1401–1464)
- Karl Rahner (1904–1984)
- Thomas Merton (1915–1968)
- Louis Dupré (1925–)

Needless to say, an introductory book cannot hope to be exhaustive.[30] Instead, like a photographer hanging up his favorite shots for an exhibition, I will provide a series of individual, related moments that are, as yet, not completely reconciled. I prefer this method—as opposed to providing my own streamlined "theory" of mysticism—for many reasons: in part, because I don't really have a streamlined theory; in part, because I think surveying a select variety of mystical treatises in some detail will keep us from too quickly reaching for easy formulas. When we keep in mind the slight discordance between Gregory's "eternal progress" and Dionysius's "God beyond being," or between Augustine's teaching on how the intellect melts into love and Merton's bleak desert, then we are forced to remember that, to a certain extent, all these "systems" and teachings are themselves metaphorical. Nothing kills the mystique of mysticism quite like finding *the* right formula. However, I am convinced that we moderns, who have come to feel that religion is some sort of process of self-improvement or inculturation into civic duty, need to recover the premodern vision of God in all its fierce joy and heartening wildness. That felt need, as it developed in the twentieth century, is what the first chapter is about.

Before turning to the first chapter, in which we will look at the unexpected reemergence of mysticism in the twentieth century, I'd like to conclude this introduction with a taste of the "strangeness" I've referred to—that is, to the alternative to our "nice" God. It comes from one of the great mystics (or visionaries) of the medieval period, Hildegard of Bingen (1098–1179). Of all the writers I will reference throughout this book, Hildegard might be the most paradigmatic exemplar of what I have referred to as "wildness." She is by turns uplifting, inspiring, provoking, and off-puttingly strange. Poet, abbess, composer, visionary, prophet, reformer, painter (maybe), and "holistic" physician, she claims to have had visions from the age of five, visions made up of strange, symbolic pictures, similar to the images that haunt the apocalyptic pages of John, Ezekiel, Isaiah, and Daniel. Hildegard records, describes, and comments on these visions in three hefty books that together constitute her magnum opus, *Scivias*.

Scivias is made up of a series of chapters, each of which begins with a description of some phantasmagorical image and then moves on to provide a moral interpretation of the image. In the

original edition, which was lost during World War II, these written descriptions were accompanied by paintings created (or at
least overseen) by Hildegard herself. The first image—as wild
as anything concocted by Picasso or Chagall—is of a mountain
of iron, with one seated upon it who is so bright that Hildegard
says she was blinded when she looked upon this figure with the
eye of her heart. From this bright one a river of sparks flows forth
and then pours out onto a figure covered in eyes who stands next
to a child wearing simple garments. After describing this vision,
Hildegard explains: the mountain represents "the strength and
stability of the eternal Kingdom of God, which no fluctuation of
mutability can destroy"; the bright one is the one who "rules the
whole world with celestial divinity in the brilliance of unfading
serenity, but is incomprehensible to human minds"; and the figure
covered in eyes represents "the fear of the Lord," which "stands in
God's presence with humility and gazes on the Kingdom of God,
surrounded by the clarity of a good and just intention, exercising
her zeal and stability among humans. . . . For by the acute sight of
her contemplation she counters all forgetfulness of God's justice,
which people often feel in their mental tedium."[31] *Scivias*, then,
is a work about being "awake" to the essence of reality, to the
secrets behind the veil: "And as the power of God is everywhere
and encompasses all things, and no obstacles can stand against
it, so too the human intellect has great power to resound in living
voices, and arouse sluggish souls to vigilance."[32]

And what is at the heart of reality? The life of God. At times
Hildegard likens it to a "living light," at other times to an eternal
symphony. In fact, over the course of her work, Hildegard's vision
is simultaneously audible and visible, a painted song and a sung
illumination (see *Scivias* 3.13). But this burning, "living light" is
at the heart of all her visions, the secret that explains the "inmost
contents of the Scriptures":

> And behold! In the forty-third year of my earthly course, as I was
> gazing with great fear and trembling attention at a heavenly vision,

I saw a great splendor in which resounded a voice from Heaven, saying to me, "O fragile human, ashes of ashes, and filth of filth! Say and write what you see and hear. . . ." Heaven was opened and a fiery light of exceeding brilliance came and permeated my whole brain, and inflamed my whole heart and my whole breast, not like a burning but like a warming flame, as the sun warms anything its rays touch. And immediately I knew the meaning of the exposition of the Scriptures.[33]

Then the voice addresses her personally:

I am the Living Light, Who illuminates the darkness. The person whom I have chosen and whom I have miraculously stricken as I willed, I have placed among great wonders, beyond the measure of the ancient people who saw in Me many secrets, but I have laid her low on the earth, that she might not set herself up in arrogance of mind. The world has had in her no joy or lewdness or use in worldly things, for I have withdrawn her from impudent boldness, and she feels fear and is timid in her works.[34]

At the heart of the world, we find the secret meaning of the universe: the life of God. All other things—political power, ambitious human projects, artistic achievements—are just dry leaves in the wind by comparison: "And I, a person not glowing with the strength of strong lions or taught by their inspiration, but a tender and fragile rib imbued with a mystical breath, saw a blazing fire, incomprehensible, inextinguishable, wholly living and wholly Life."[35] This sickly, timid woman, this broken vessel chosen because of its fragility, dared to raise her voice to instruct the powerful men of her era: emperor, abbots, bishops, and pope. Like other female mystics considered in this book (Julian of Norwich and Angela of Foligno), Hildegard, on the periphery of society, a "mere woman" and inheritor of the "curse of Eve," was chosen precisely because of her fragility: "Burst forth into a fountain of abundance and overflow with mystical knowledge, until they who now think you contemptible because of Eve's transgression are stirred up by the flood of your irrigation. For you have received your profound insight not from humans, but from the lofty and tremendous Judge on high, where this calmness will shine strongly with glorious light among the shining ones."[36]

When we keep in mind Hildegard's vision of the inextinguishable fire, we can understand why a much earlier mystic, Gregory the Great (540–604), in his commentary on Job could say that the ascent to God was one of mingled joy and terror. Commenting on part of Eliphaz's speech to Job ("Now a thing was secretly brought to me, and mine ear received a little thereof. In thoughts from the visions of the night, when deep sleep falleth on men, fear came upon me, and trembling, which made all my bones to shake," Job 4:12–14), Gregory says this:

> The dread of a nocturnal vision is the trembling caused by hidden contemplation. The more elevated the human mind becomes by the consideration of eternity, the more intense is its fear and trembling over its earthly deeds. . . . It so happens that enlightenment causes it to fear the more, because it sees much better how far it falls short from the rule of truth.[37]

It is this vision of God that the mystics I discuss below felt they were called to keep safe—a searing, wild vision of a God who cannot be imprisoned within the order he created. I now turn to exploring how, in the wasteland of the twentieth century, there was a renewed desire to bring it back.

1

The Christian of the Future
in the Desert of Modernity

The Twentieth-Century Rediscovery of Ancient Mysticism

I n the introduction I talked about the glacial spiritual shift that
has moved through the centuries of modernity and fundamentally altered the spiritual landscape in which we live. It's not
that (as some might wish) the new science and modern political
order ended religion. As Charles Taylor and others have pointed
out, even today you can have a "spin" on the world as open to
God, or a "spin" on the world as closed: that is, those vast cosmic
spaces, which we all know about, can be read as a sign of God's
majestic mind or as a cosmic wasteland, in which case we have to
get over God and move on with the project of perfecting ourselves.[1]

In this chapter, though, I want to talk about how, in the twentieth century, the ancient practice of mysticism rather unexpectedly
began to seem like something urgently needed by modern souls.
In a world of skyscrapers and computers and electricity, the writings (often surviving only in fragments) of men and women from
a distant age, whose habits of mind were so foreign to our own,

25

suddenly were seen to be steeped in a wisdom that was desperately needed. In what follows, we'll first discuss the desertlike conditions of the twentieth century; then I'll turn to three twentieth-century Christian authors who drew attention to the modern need to recover mysticism, and the reasons they gave for mysticism's unexpected contemporary relevance.

The Silence of God in the Twentieth Century

By the beginning of the twentieth century, God, even if not completely "dead," was at least no longer indubitably obvious. The fermentation process of secularization had already been at work for several hundred years. But over the course of the twentieth century in particular, the feeling of being lost intensified, and it became a major theme in art and music and literature. This was the age of Penderecki's *Threnody for the Victims of Hiroshima*, eight minutes of pained screeching on fifty-two stringed instruments; this was the age of Messiaen's *Quartet for the End of Time* as well as of Spengler's *The Downfall of the Occident* (1918). Achilles, Odysseus, Lancelot, and the pilgrim (both Bunyan's and Dante's) were replaced by J. Alfred Prufrock, Holden Caulfield, Don Draper, Binx Bolling (in Walker Percy's *The Moviegoer*), and Hemingway's lost men: souls of great capacity who wander throughout the world, like ghosts, looking for a place to incarnate in. But they can't because they can't shake the suspicion that everything is "phony" (to borrow Holden's favorite word). Dupré put it this way: "Ours is an anemic culture whose members have become listless and tired."[2]

By the beginning of the twentieth century, many had concluded that the West was now definitively bankrupt. The infinitely fascinating and strange René Guénon (1886–1951), for example, who later converted to Sufism, writing in the midst of the European avant-garde movement, preached that modern civilization does not follow the pattern of evolution but is, rather, going backward. Labeling the modern world "the Dark Age," Guénon, like his contemporary, the French painter Paul Gauguin, felt that Europe was utterly exhausted:

> The truths which were formerly within reach of all have become more and more hidden and inaccessible; those who possess them grow fewer and fewer, and although the treasure of "nonhuman" (that is, supra-human) wisdom that was prior to all the ages can never be lost, it nevertheless becomes enveloped in more and more impenetrable veils, which hide it from men's sight and make it extremely difficult to discover. This is why we find everywhere, under various symbols, the same theme of something that has been lost.[3]

A chorus of social critics agreed with Guénon. John Burroughs referred to the age as suffering from "the cosmic chill"; T. S. Eliot called it a "waste land"; Susan Taubes referenced "the absent God"; Karl Rahner talked about a spiritual "winter" (see below); and contemporary philosopher Michael Rea likes to use the term "divine hiddenness" to sum up the spiritual condition of modernity.[4] Similarly, Flannery O'Connor, writing to a friend who was struggling with faith, said that "there are long periods in the lives of all of us, and of the saints, when the truth as revealed by faith is hideous, emotionally disturbing, downright repulsive. Witness the dark night of the soul in individual saints. Right now the whole world seems to be going through a dark night of the soul."[5] Even John Henry Newman, writing in the nineteenth century, presciently summed up the feeling that would undergo an outbreak in the next century: "What strikes the mind so forcibly and so painfully is, [God's] absence (if I may so speak) from His own world. It is a silence that speaks. It is as if others had got possession of His work. Why does not He, our Maker and Ruler, give us some immediate knowledge of Himself?" In the sermon "Waiting for Christ," Newman describes this alienation even more poignantly:

> He is still here; He still whispers to us, He still makes signs to us. But his voice is so low, and the world's din is so loud, and His

signs are so covert, and the world is so restless, that it is difficult
to determine when He addresses us, and what He says. Religious
men cannot but feel . . . that his providence is guiding them, . . .
yet when they attempt to put their finger upon times and places,
the traces of His presence disappear.[6]

Shūsaku Endō

Perhaps the most painful portrait of this landscape of divine
desolation is found in Shūsaku Endō's *Silence* (published as *Chin-
moku* in 1966). Endō subtly projects twentieth-century anxieties
back onto seventeenth-century Japan through the fictional life and
death of the Portuguese Jesuit missionary Fr. Sebastião Rodrigues.

Throughout *Silence* the intuitive, reflective, and idealistic Jesuit
priest has contempt for apostate Christians such as the groveling,
Judas-like Kichijirō because they lack strength of will. But Rodrigues is unsettled by a growing anxiety. All his life, he wanted
nothing more than to practice his priestly faculties: to lead the
prayers of the liturgy, to hear confessions, to sing in public processions, to erect ornate Baroque churches worthy of God. But now, in
the "swamps of Japan," the priest has to go into hiding immediately
after arriving, and, when discovered, he goes on the run, furtively
moving from hiding spot to hiding spot in the mountains until he
is finally betrayed by Kichijirō to the authorities. The authorities
have a special type of torture in mind for Rodrigues. Rather than
harming him, they offer him silk clothes, a house, a concubine, and
a quiet life dedicated to the writing of ennobling books. All they ask
is that he set his foot on an image of Christ, a "mere formality." If
he does not apostatize, the officials promise to torture and execute
the simple peasants who look to him for guidance.

When the first of these peasants are rounded up and put to
death, hung on a cross for days on a part of the beach where the
tides submerge them up to their chins, Kichijirō turns to Fr. Rodrigues and asks, "Father . . . what evil have we done?" Rodrigues
later reflects on the question:

I suppose I should simply cast from my mind these meaningless words of the coward; yet why does his plaintive voice pierce my breast with all the pain of a sharp needle? Why has Our Lord imposed this torture and this persecution on poor Japanese peasants? No, Kichijirō was trying to express something different, something even more sickening. The silence of God. Already twenty years have passed since the persecution broke out; the black soil of Japan has been filled with the lament of so many Christians; the red blood of priests has flowed profusely; the walls of the churches have fallen down; and in the face of this terrible and merciless sacrifice offered up to Him, God has remained silent. This was the problem that lay behind the plaintive question of Kichijirō.[7]

Rodrigues tries to shake it off, but over the course of the book, the world feels more and more empty to him, to the point that he begins to worry that he is losing his faith. The banality of the deaths of the peasants is so unlike the glorious Baroque paintings of martyrs from back home. And everything is just so silent. Rodrigues keeps returning to this monotonous silence as he reflects on the deaths of the peasants:

> They were martyred. But what a martyrdom! I had long read about martyrdom in the lives of the saints—how the souls of the martyrs had gone home to Heaven, how they had been filled with glory in Paradise, how the angels had blown trumpets. This was the splendid martyrdom I had often seen in my dreams. But the martyrdom of the Japanese Christians I now describe to you was no such glorious thing. What a miserable and painful business it was! The rain falls unceasingly on the sea. And the sea which killed them surges on uncannily—in silence. . . . Behind the depressing silence of this sea, the silence of God . . . the feeling that while men raise their voices in anguish God remains with folded arms, silent.[8]

Always in the background is the sea, that symbol of unresponsive silence.[9] On the run, Rodrigues enters a town of "empty desolation,"[10] pillaged by officials searching for Christians. On the run, the priest keeps turning back to look at the sea. And over the course of the novel, he is stripped of more and more practices of the faith. He loses track of time and thus loses access to the liturgy.[11] He has no access to bread and wine, and so he loses access to the Mass. He even starts to lose access to the words of the old prayers: "'Exaudi nos, Pater omnipotens . . . ' Repeating the prayer again and again he tried wildly to distract his attention; but the prayer could not tranquillize his agonized heart. 'Lord, why are you silent? Why are you always silent . . . ?'"[12]

The breaking point for poor Rodrigues is when Ferreira, his beloved teacher from seminary who had apostatized years before, confronts him. Rodrigues still remembers him with affection and admiration, not having seen him since he was a student. And so when Ferreira comes back into Rodrigues's life and in his stern, fatherly way utters aloud the doubts of his soul, Rodrigues crumbles:

> Ferreira raised a voice that was like a growl as he shouted: "The reason I apostatized . . . are you ready? Listen! I was put in here and heard the voices of those people for whom God did nothing. God did not do a single thing. I prayed with all my strength; but God did nothing." . . .
>
> [Rodrigues] shook his head wildly, putting both fingers into his ears. But the voice of Ferreira together with the groaning of the Christians broke mercilessly in. Stop! Stop! Lord, it is now that you should break the silence. You must not remain silent. Prove that you are justice, that you are goodness, that you are love. You must say something to show the world that you are the august one.[13]

In the end, Rodrigues fails, and he tramples the face of Christ, which had been so dear to him throughout his life. Strange as it may sound, Endō's novel is actually a novel of deep faith. It might be read, then, as the biography of a near saint, a figure who almost found Christ in the midst of desolation. But Endō's genius has to do with the background of the priest's failure, what was variously called, in the twentieth century, divine desolation, divine hiddenness, divine silence, divine emptiness, practical atheism, or a-theism—the lived condition in which the nearness of God has seemed to evaporate.

Rudolf Otto

In the twentieth century, plagued by everything from a piercing sense of abandonment to a lazy spiritual lassitude, many thinkers became restless and began to ask what the alternatives were. A series of scholars began to excavate experiences of religion from the premodern world, in which God seemed more obvious and close and ubiquitous. For example, the German scholar Rudolf Otto, who published his *The Idea of the Holy* in 1917, argued that modern people have lost a sense of what the holy is. Otto coined the term "numinous" to get at what he believed we have lost: "There is no religion in which [the numinous] does not live as the real innermost core, and without it no religion would be worthy of the name."[14] For Otto, the numinous is that reality whose majesty is so far beyond our ordinary experience that it is difficult for us to classify it simply as good or bad; it is at once both alluring and dangerous, beautiful and terrifying, like Ezekiel's experience of God in Ezekiel 1.

To describe this lost experience of the sacred in the ancient world, Otto said that the numinous has five characteristics. It is *mysterium*; it possesses *maiestas*; it is *tremendum*; it contains an "urgent energy"; and it is *fascinans*. A *mysterium* is literally a "mystery" or a "secret," but not in the way we ordinarily use those words. A mystery novel leaves you puzzled (like a detective story) until you figure out the missing piece. But a true mystery never loses its question-provoking nature, even when you learn more about it. It inspires a response of "stupor," "blank wonder, an astonishment that strikes us dumb, amazement absolute" (26). The numinous is also *mysterium tremendum*—that is, a mystery that causes fear, religious dread, and awe. It is uncanny. It causes you to shudder, like the weird sisters in Macbeth do, because it seems to be on a different plane of being. But unlike the weird sisters, that which is supremely numinous possesses "dread majesty" (*maiestas*), an overpowering unapproachability. Otto also says that the numinous has an "urgent energy," as if it is on the verge of pouring forth. According to Otto, the mystics refer to this aspect when they write about the "consuming fire" of God, "whose burning strength the mystic can hardly bear, but begs that the heat that has scorched him may be mitigated, lest he be himself destroyed by it" (24). But at the same time, Otto says, the numinous is *mysterium fascinans*: "[It] may appear to the mind an object of horror and dread, but at the same time it is no less something that allures with a potent charm, and the creature, who trembles before it, utterly cowed and cast down, has always at the same time the impulse to turn to it, nay even to make it somehow his own. The 'mystery' is for him not merely something to be wondered at but something that entrances him" (31).

All these properties exist simultaneously in the numinous: it is frightening, imposing, powerful, and wondrous. It feels that it is rushing out, while at the same time drawing you in. For this reason it inspires *dread* in the creature who comes into contact with it. This is exactly what we find in the Old Testament, when Isaiah is given a vision of God, seated enthroned in his holiness (Isa. 6). Isaiah's vision is an experience of awe and terror and fullness. In sum, as Otto puts it, "a god comprehended is no God" (26).

Mircea Eliade (1907–1986)

Another example of a twentieth-century writer acting as an archaeologist of ancient forms of religion is the Romanian historian Mircea Eliade, whose most famous book is *The Sacred and the Profane*. Eliade built on Otto's work by arguing that moments of encounter with the numinous were the sociological cornerstone of "primitive" or "archaic" societies: "For religious man, space is not homogeneous; he experiences interruptions, breaks in it;

some parts of space are qualitatively different from others."[15] Needless to say, in contemporary American culture we are about as far away from this mindset as possible. For us, empty land is a resource, waiting for buildings, waiting to yield its resources, waiting to be turned into a housing development. We have no notion that some land is different; in Eliade's terms, all space for us is homogeneous.

But this was not the case for people in the archaic world, whom he calls *homo religiosus*. Some tracts of land had been broken open, as it were, in order for divinity to manifest itself. Where this happens is not the will of human beings but the will of the god or goddess. This space now becomes set apart because of the "irruption of the sacred that results in detaching a territory from the surrounding cosmic milieu and making it qualitatively different."[16] This is hard for us to believe in. Eliade says that "profane man" "finds it difficult to accept the fact that, for many human beings, the sacred can be manifested in stones or trees, for example. But . . . what is involved is not a veneration of the stone in itself, a cult of the tree in itself. The sacred tree, the sacred stone are not adored as stone or tree; they are worshipped precisely because they are *hierophanies*, because they show something that is no longer stone or tree but the *sacred*."[17] If this is beginning to sound too creepy and New Agey, just recall the many instances in Genesis in which Abraham and Jacob encounter God. The sites of those encounters are commemorated with altars and named. Moses had an encounter with a sacred bush, too: "Draw not nigh hither: put off thy shoes from off thy feet, for the place whereon thou standest is holy ground" (Exod. 3:5).

Eliade goes on to explain that ancient people oriented entire societies around these sacred spaces; their lives were centered on the sacred. In other words, they didn't just build shrines and, later, temples but rather created their cities to radiate out from these religious sites in order to facilitate an ongoing encounter with the sacred. Without the sacred to orient *homo religiosus*, they feel lost and disoriented. Ancient people, then, were radically rooted in a place, and they couldn't just pick up and move (think of how reluctant Aeneas was to be uprooted from Troy). Everywhere else was a nonplace, a place lacking meaning.[18]

Look, for example, at an aerial view of Durham, England, and notice how the town is a harmonious blend of sacred architecture, houses and businesses orbiting the cathedral, all surrounded by natural places. Heidelberg, Germany, and York, England, and towns in Umbria and Tuscany, Italy, present similar cases. But while many European cities resemble the old view of the cosmos, with buildings literally radiating out from their religious centers, modern cities betray their anticosmic individualism. If you drive through Dallas, that modern city par excellence (and a city I really like, by the way), you will find not a harmonious cosmos but a collection of individually wrought buildings competing for your attention. Dallas was built in the world of homogenized space.

A sense of loss, then, made up the broad context for the twentieth-century recovery of Christian mysticism. Many intellectuals worried more and more that spiritual poverty was too high a price to pay for economic prosperity, and they wondered whether gaining technological control over the natural world was worth the loss of meaning that came with it.[19] During the years when brutal, mechanized wars ravaged Europe, wars that eventually scarred Asia and Africa as well; during the years in which highly sophisticated, Wagner-listening nations used their unparalleled scientific achievements to shred, scorch, and poison the flesh of farm boys from the countryside—during these years there was born a desire to see what could be retrieved from the past (a *post*modern recovery).[20] From the vantage point of the "anemic" twentieth century (Dupré's term), the ancient and medieval world looked so robust, so "God-filled," so much closer to spiritual realities. Thus many during those years of disillusionment became nostalgic for what had been lost. And it is in this context that the teachings of the Christian mystics, although bizarre and foreign and otherworldly, seemed to offer a special word of consolation for a world that had been stripped of ritual, morality, and the presence of God. To some, mysticism seemed to offer a way of return.

Even for the second half of the twentieth century, less stricken
by shocking displays of human cruelty but, rather, suffocating
in the malaise of meaningless, hyperactive commerce, mysticism
held out the promise of depth, interiority, and authenticity. What
Louis Dupré called a "benign atheism" had set in: "Today's
atheism by and large considers its position sufficiently secure
to feel no need for defining itself through a negative relation
to faith."[21] And so, for the first time in human history, it was
possible to spend your whole life not just without encountering
God but without even knowing you were supposed to. In the
late twentieth century, then, in a world of banality and com-
mercialized religion in which God had become "nice," mysticism
promised to help "unchain" God from the small, moralistic
demands laid on him—to let God be wild and free and daring
and beautiful.[22] In short, for the last one hundred years mysticism has "haunted" modernity, as the Jesuit Michel de Certeau
once put it. Mysticism is the "wild science" that frightens the
domesticated ones.[23]

   In the rest of this chapter I want to look at three authors who
believed that mysticism had something that the twentieth century
urgently needed. I'll start with Thomas Merton's understanding
of silence. For modern people, Merton thought, "silence" means
merely the cessation of noise; but what he admired so much about
the ancient, contemplative tradition was its *positive* understanding
of silence—that is, that it could be a kind of "pregnant silence"
in which one can "hear" the world's deep meaning. Then I'll turn
to the writings of Karl Rahner and Louis Dupré and their belief
that the spiritual desert of modernity could, under the right conditions of faith, be transformed into a uniquely modern path to
holiness—not just despite its bleakness but because of it! Rahner
and Dupré thought that we need to own our modernity, to deal
with it, to lean into its desolation, and to trust that by doing so a
new, leaner, deeper, more vital closeness to God will be the result.
Twentieth-century cultural conditions, then, provided the desert
our ancestors had to seek out.

Silence as Antidote to Noise

For those spiritual writers born toward the end of the nineteenth century, and who lived into the mid-twentieth century, the single most disturbing change between their childhoods and their mature, adult lives was the advent of the incessant world of noise. Born into the last days of a time in which news arrived by post, they soon found themselves thrust into an age of electricity, engines, flight, and speed. It was a profound transformation, difficult for us who are born "digital" (or at least "electric") to imagine. Max Picard, C. S. Lewis, Dorothy Sayers, Romano Guardini, Thomas Merton, Karl Rahner, and Josef Pieper, as well as the American Southern Agrarians, all felt that the incessant clatter of modern progress had tremendously negative effects on the spiritual psyche of the worlds they lived in. The new world of radios, telephones, televisions, skyscrapers, automobiles, interstates, instantaneity, and petroleum-fueled power gave modern people the opportunity to live on the periphery of their being. All day long, they could allow themselves to be occupied by an endless stream of tasks and concerns and desires implanted by advertisers. And they were told by their governments and corporations to respond with bustle and pep. You couldn't, perhaps, outrun yourself, but you could move so fast you'd at least forget who you really were. Indeed, Lewis thought that this was one of the four biggest changes in human history.[24]

In some ways this culture of noise and fidgeting was a long time coming. Its roots were put down two centuries earlier, when the traditional understanding of a person as a contemplative being (*homo theoreticus*) turned into "man the worker" (*homo faber*), a creature who must realize

> himself exclusively through work and who *makes* himself while *making* his world. . . . The contemplative ideal has been abandoned for an active one—whether it be the constitutive activity of consciousness or the technical activity of man—which allows the mind to impose its structure on the world. Max Scheler regards this

anticontemplative attitude of the West (present in its religion as well as in its science and technology) as the triumph of the practical Roman spirit over the more theoretical Greek-Oriental one.[25]

The important thing to emphasize is that what was revolutionary in the nineteenth century (the transition from *homo theoreticus* to *homo faber*) had become banal by the age of *Mad Men*. And no one was more allergic to this banality than Thomas Merton, the onetime bohemian intellectual and poet who, after converting to Catholicism, became a Trappist monk at Gethsemani Abbey in Kentucky. But throughout his life he was alert to our tendency in modernity to live life on the periphery of our being, to fidget, and to clutter our minds and bodies with superfluity. In his great autobiography, *The Seven Storey Mountain*, Merton looks back with disgust on his habit of chain smoking, his restless bouncing from place to place, his spiritual hyperactivity. He declares that a dovecote made in medieval France is more beautiful than a one-hundred-million-dollar American university. In a piece his editors called "Mysticism in the Nuclear Age," Merton gives this assessment of the inherent restlessness of the modern age: "We fling ourselves into activities that are supposed to change the world and ourselves with it. . . . But the forces thus released are changing the world into one that is no longer Christian."[26] Ever allergic to the clichés of his age, he adds,

> The world we live in is dry ground for the seed of God's Truth. A modern American city is not altogether a propitious place in which to try to love God. You cannot love Him unless you know Him. And you cannot come to know Him unless you have a little time and a little peace in which to pray and think about Him and study His truth. Time and peace are not easily come by in this civilization of ours. (372)

Despite his pessimism, Merton was convinced that, in this world in which the masks have been torn off—in which "we have

awakened to our fundamental barbarism"—there is, paradoxically, "once again a hope for civilization" (374). By this he means
that because "our tremendous capacities for evil [stare] us in the
face, there is more incentive than ever for men to become saints"
(374). In an almost Augustinian fashion, our very restlessness has
created the possibility for us to have a renewed thirst for God.
Because even "morality" can no longer be taken for granted, we
are in a position in which we have to ask why we should be good
in the first place: "Virtue, for a Christian, is not its own reward"
(375). But that restlessness makes us want something deeper and
fuller and more potent—something that can ground us and help
us return from the periphery of our being to a deeper interior
life. Merton again:

> Our ordinary waking life is a bare existence in which, most of the
> time, we seem to be absent from ourselves and from reality because
> we are involved in the vain preoccupations which dog the steps of
> every living man. But there are times when we seem suddenly to
> awake and discover the full meaning of our own present reality.
> Such discoveries are not capable of being contained in formulas
> or definitions. They are a matter of personal experience, of un-
> communicable intuition. In the light of such an experience it is
> easy to see the futility of all the trifles that occupy our minds. We
> recapture something of the calm and balance that ought always
> to be ours, and we understand that life is far too great a gift to be
> squandered on anything less than perfection. (376–77)

It is this psychic fatigue and harried feeling, this reluctance to
turn an inner eye to the shallowness of our own souls, that makes
us—perhaps like no other generation before—positively desire
what Merton elsewhere calls the solitude of the desert. Our tired
modernity makes us thirsty for depth. And for this reason, Merton's words on silence are hypnotically enchanting.

As I have noted, the chief feature of silence for Merton (as well
as for his German contemporary Max Picard)[27] is that silence is

something positive, a form of communion with something beyond the frontiers of language: "[In solitude] we communicate with Him alone, without words, without discursive thoughts, in the silence of our whole being."[28] For Merton, such "positive" silence can and should become the new core of our morality. We do good things and participate in traditional morality, not because we are afraid of the social consequences of not doing so or because it is good to follow rules, but because this is a way of preserving our ability to be in tune with the world, to be in tune with God, and to be in harmony with those around us: "Silence is the strength of our interior life. Silence enters into the very core of our moral being, so that if we have no silence we have no morality. Silence enters mysteriously into the composition of all the virtues, and silence preserves them from corruption."[29]

Thus, there is an *inner* stillness that opens us up to hear the *outer* silence of the world: "If you go into solitude with a silent tongue, the silence of mute beings will share with you their rest."[30] Merton is here, in his terse, modern, poetic prose, recycling the traditional teaching of "natural contemplation," which enjoyed a long history from the desert fathers down through nineteenth-century Russia (see chap. 5 below). But what the ancients knew intimately, in their bones, has become foreign to us who "love our own noise": "Those who love their own noise are impatient of everything else. They constantly defile the silence of the forests and the mountains and the sea. They bore through silent nature in every direction with their machines, for fear that the calm world might accuse them of their own emptiness."[31] But those of us brave enough to endure the accusation, and to look with sorrow at the shambles of our interior lives, will find that a new phase of depth and love and authenticity can begin.[32]

Merton's words are strangely hypnotic, but he's not alone in describing the positive opportunities that the spiritual desert of modernity presents. Karl Rahner and Louis Dupré take up a similar theme.

Karl Rahner and Louis Dupré on the Uses of the Desert

Karl Rahner, the German Jesuit theologian, and Louis Dupré, the Belgian-born intellectual historian, each took a bold step beyond Merton. If Merton believed that we could recover the wisdom and practices of the past despite the obstacles of modernity, Rahner and Dupré thought that we could do so *because of* or *through* the conditions of modern desolation. Both Rahner and Dupré were insistent that not even the believer can escape modernity or pretend to belong to a past age, however much one wishes to. It is not possible to escape the background music of "divine silence." Rahner writes, "We live in a world in which man has made even his own interior life the subject of technical scientific investigation, . . . a world . . . in which the suspicion is never absent from his mind that his religious experience may be unmasked as an outmoded and erroneous interpretation of psychological drives, needs and processes which can and must be explained and brought under control by quite different means than through a mystical and indefinite entity called 'God.'"[33] Similarly, Dupré was insistent that we cannot turn back the clock: "I do not regard a simple revival of ancient beliefs and traditional institutions *in itself* as a solution to any of today's problems. . . . In fact, all too often they form one of the main obstacles on the road to genuine transcendence."[34] And Rahner adds that, whereas our ancestors might have been able to enjoy the "luxury" of "elaborate systems of devotion," we have to reconcile ourselves to the fact that "in this wintry season, the tree of . . . devotion cannot be expected to bear such an abundance of leaves and blooms in the form of the various devotions and pious practices of the past."[35]

Both Rahner and Dupré presciently predicted an age in which there would no longer be any cultural Christians. Any form of Christianity that did not draw deeply from within would wither away. And yet there is consolation in this: although in modernity God has been "lowered to a scale of being where he can no longer be truly sacred,"[36] we abide in an age that has pulled off the mask of this fake god: "Until recently, the process of decomposition was hidden by the unmoving mask of a traditional god to whom we continued to pay lip service. Now at last the mask has been torn off and behind it stares the emptiness of the abyss."[37] Because religion has suffered this social collapse, "in a secularized society the religious person has nowhere to turn but inward. There, and for the most part there alone, must he seek support for his religious attitude."[38] In other words, the desolation, the silence, could paradoxically bring about a new spiritual depth in which we have to push our roots way down deep or die in the winter. Rahner's inspiring words address the peculiar difficulties of living in the great age of divine silence:

> Today anyone who manages to live with this incomprehensible and silent God is already practising devout Christian living. One who finds courage to call upon him ever anew, to speak to him in a spirit of faith, trust and patience in his darkness, even though to all appearances no answer is returned except the hollow echo of his own voice—such a one as this is already a devout Christian. If a man repeatedly empties himself of all else so as to open himself to the depths of his being to the incomprehensibility of God [and] ... if he still manages to live with God and commune with him in spite of this and without the support of "public opinion" and custom, then he is already a devout Christian.[39]

And so both Rahner and Dupré imagine a new, raw, stripped-down piety that has a "modern" devotion to two things: "the incomprehensibility of God and his effective presence in the crucified one, the one abandoned by God."[40] If, in the twentieth century (as now), we were tempted to commoditize religion and make God "work for me," the spreading pandemic of spiritual desolation removed this false consolation, and made us either wither or seek renewal. In other words, the desert of desolation of modernity keeps us from trying to "name" God—that is, to label or categorize too easily the Ineffable One. Modernity helps us recover an ancient sense of the numinous.

Dupré also suggested that our world, precisely by depriving us of the comforting presence of God, could create a landscape in which we have to heroically face the absence—but that doing so would allow for the possibility of God's being to recede far beyond the horizons of our idolizing images of him. Dupré calls this "vitalizing the negative experience":

> Since the third century the mystical tradition of Christianity has recognized a theology in which all language is reduced to silence. In his *Mystical Theology*, Pseudo-Dionysius, the sixth-century Syrian monk, teaches that all striving for spiritual perfection must abandon all experience, all concepts and all objects, to be united with what lies beyond all cognition: "Into this Dark beyond all light, we pray to come, and unseeing and unknowing to see and know Him that is beyond seeing and beyond knowing precisely by not seeing, by not knowing . . ." Clearly a negation such as [this] did not emerge from a weakened religious consciousness, but, quite the opposite, from a more intensive religious awareness, which is missing in our contemporaries. Yet my point . . . is to show that if the believer, who shares in fact, if not in principle, the practical a-theism of his entire culture, is left no other choice but to vitalize this negative experience and to confront his feeling of God's absence, he may find himself on the very road walked by spiritual pilgrims in more propitious times. What was once the arduous road travelled only by a religious elite is now in many instances the only one still open to us. . . . The desert of modern atheism provides the only space in which most of us are forced to encounter the transcendent. . . . Our age has created an emptiness that in the serious God-seeker attains a religious significance.[41]

For both Rahner and Dupré, ancient traditions are relevant again because they provide us with a paradigm in which God could be unchained from his creation: "But what the believer encounters in himself is in the first place the silence of absence—a silence in which God's word no longer resounds and in which creatures have ceased to speak the sacred language. The believer has no choice but to enter into that silence. In the confrontation with his own a-theism, accepting the emptiness in his own heart, he acquires the sacred 'sense of absence' of which Simone Weil wrote."[42]

In the remainder of this book, we will see that the words I have quoted from Merton, Rahner, and Dupré are echoes of the ancient "negative" (or apophatic) theology of mysticism, the practice by which we "unsay" what God is in order to restore in our minds the possibility that he is above our human conceptions. We can't commoditize God, make faith easy, or let it become a "useful" and easy part of our personalities. In this sense, we can't "name" God. In our age, it will no longer be enough to hold right doctrines and follow traditional morality. We'll need something more: "The devout Christian of the future will either be a 'mystic' . . . or he will cease to be anything at all."[43]

2

Pagans Grope toward God

Piety and Prayer in Antiquity

Vain is the word of that philosopher which does not heal any suffering man.
—Epicurean saying

The pagan accounts of the good life often lacked the drama
of the biblical narratives. In contrast to the wandering of
the Israelites through the desert, whose bitter experiences
are continually being turned into object lessons (e.g., the bronze
serpent; Moses striking rocks; the reception of stone tablets from
God; the destruction of the golden calf), the lives of Socrates,
Plato, Aristotle, the Stoics, and, later, Plotinus are fairly sedentary.
Their lives consist in friendship, conversation, dialectic, and grad-
ual training in the moral virtues. Plato likens the philosophical life
to the tedious process of rubbing sticks together to get them hot
enough to cause a spark: "Only when all of these things—names,
definitions, and visual and other perceptions—have been rubbed
against one another and tested, pupil and teacher asking and

answering questions in good will and without envy—only then, when reason and knowledge are at the very extremity of human effort, can they illuminate the nature of any object" ("Seventh Letter" 344b; compare *Republic* 435a).[1] Similarly, Plotinus talks about the philosophical life as involving years of patient, detailed work in which we polish and hone and chip away at our interior lives, as if we were painstakingly carving a statue. And famously, Socrates had an encounter with the supernatural, the so-called divine sign that he describes in the *Apology*; but, rather prosaically, his guardian *daimon* would only speak to him when he was *not* supposed to do something.[2] Compelled by a sincere desire to know and be just, though, Socrates explains to his jurors that he cannot stop his persistent search: "If I say that it is impossible for me to keep quiet because that means disobeying the god, you will not believe me and will think I am being ironical. On the other hand, if I say that it is the greatest good for a man to discuss virtue every day and those other things about which you hear me conversing and testing myself and others, for the unexamined life is not worth living for men, you will believe me even less" (*Apology* 38a). Contrast how Socrates describes his life (conversation, thinking, tinkering with virtues) with the description of the enveloping presence of God in Exodus: "I will do marvels, such as have not been done in all the earth, . . . for it is a terrible thing that I will do with thee" (Exod. 34:10). We note the difference.

Unlike the fulminating, history-changing irruptions of the divine in the Bible, the Greek search for God was more like groping in the dark: quieter, shot through with questions and doubt, more interior—more like, as Plotinus puts it, straining to hear a whispering voice: "It is as if someone was expecting to hear a voice which he wanted to hear and withdrew from other sounds and roused his power of hearing to catch what, when it comes, is the best of all sounds which can be heard" (*Enneads* V.1.12).[3] The pagan search for God was made up of doubt-filled seeking and difficult attempts to get explanations. Plato says that it's hard for truth to take hold even in a good soul, even when you have at hand all of the necessary philosophical tools.[4] Nothing is obvious; nothing is easy; truth is fugitive.

Imagine Socrates going around Athens, eager to speak with anyone who is even half willing to speak with him! He talks about artistic inspiration with Ion, piety with Euthyphro, justice with old Cephalus (in the *Republic*). Imagine, too, Diogenes cynically walking around Athens with a lantern in the middle of the day because he is looking for one just man and having trouble finding him. Such pagan groping could be described as two steps forward and one step back. If the pagan search for God—hesitant and uncertain, careful and attentive—lacked the drama of the biblical accounts of divine revelation, it at least had a certain systematic quality. Those who are lost will leave markers in the woods to help them find their way. Similarly, the Greeks, eager to retain and make permanent their hard-won insights, were systematic builders, formulators, and term-users who tried to keep everything philosophically straight. In this way they could retrace their steps if they had to. These features of classical antiquity—systematic intensity combined with sincere and intense interiority—come out most memorably in the great myths of Plato, which so nourished Plotinus.[5]

And so, even without access to revelation, the Greek philosophers were nevertheless able to grope toward God and holiness, to long for it with an intense desire for righteousness.[6] Socrates begins and ends his dialogues in prayer.[7] In his last words he reminds his friends not to forget an offering to the gods (*Phaedo* 118a). He's reverent regarding old pious tales (*Phaedrus* 229c–e) and alert to the presence of divinity in sacred landscapes (*Phaedrus* 238d). Even when he's unsure about the answers, he feels it his sacred duty to defend justice against those who cynically deny its existence: "I don't see how I can be of help. Indeed, I believe I'm incapable of it. . . . On the other hand, I don't see how I can refuse my help, for I fear that I may even be impious to have breath in one's body and the ability to speak and yet to stand idly by and not defend justice when it's being prosecuted. So the best course is to give justice any assistance I can" (*Republic* 368b). And toward the end of his life, he feels an inexplicable groaning to plunge into the darkness of the afterlife to discover what's there (e.g., *Phaedo* 114c). It is this weariless optimism, this tireless desire to get to the bottom of things and to reject merely conventional understandings, that I want to explore in the next two sections.

Plato *Mysticus*

Plato's philosophical writings are preserved in the form of dialogues, written conversations between (almost always) Socrates and "ordinary" folk in Athens (e.g., teachers of rhetoric, lawyers, old men, friends, ambitious politicians). A dialogue often begins with a chance encounter in the streets, such as when Socrates runs into Phaedrus, who is just about to leave the city walls for a country walk (*Phaedrus* 227a), or Euthyphro, who is outside the law courts (*Euthyphro* 2a), or Polemarchus, returning with a group of friends from a public parade and festival at the Piraeus (*Republic* 327a). After pleasantries are exchanged and quick questions answered ("What are you doing here?" "Where are you going?"), Socrates's interlocutor inevitably lets slip some opinion. Socrates, who is legitimately curious about everything, seizes on the half-thought-out statement and asks, "I couldn't help but notice that you just happened to refer in passing to justice [or piety or love or beauty], a subject I am keenly interested in and yet can't seem to nail down exactly what it is. Before we move on in our conversation, would you mind telling me exactly what you mean by *that*?" The interlocutor, a little perplexed and put off by the somewhat socially awkward question, is nevertheless willing to oblige, and so he airily tosses out a quick answer to Socrates's question. Over the remainder of the dialogue, Socrates pushes and pulls at the definition with question after question in pursuit of a definition that will "stand still." He asks if it applies in this situation but not in that and so forth, until the original definition completely unravels. Many of these dialogues end with the central question left unresolved (these are the "aporetic" dialogues because they end in a state of aporia, "unresolved confusion"), and the interlocutors leave in frustration or anger—although, ironically, their confidence in their ability to pronounce judgments on lofty matters generally remains unshaken. To them, it's Socrates's fault that he can't see good common sense when it stands before him.

It might have been the case that Plato wrote these dialogues as public recruiting tools. Unlike the confident interlocutors who do not like to be questioned, some readers, he might have hoped, would sincerely puzzle over the problems and worry about not being able to come up with the answers. Such readers could apply to become members of Plato's Academy, a kind of holistic school that made its members work out physically, seek piety in religious ritual, and become masters of dialectic and rigorous mathematical thinking. Once these students had achieved purity of mind and heart, they would be ready to revisit the questions that had hooked them in the first place.

In a few dialogues, though—the ones considered to be the greatest—we might have hints of the "secret" teachings reserved for the members of the inner circle of the Academy. The elusive form of question and answer ensures that Plato is never completely forthright with what he is up to; but sometimes, as we will see, in dialogues such as the *Republic*, *Phaedrus*, and *Symposium*, we do get a hint of something beyond.

Take the *Republic* as an example, that sustained inquiry of several hundred pages. At one point Socrates compares the interlocutors' search for the meaning of justice to hunting for an animal that has hidden itself in a wild forest. As Socrates almost accidentally pokes around here and there, he eventually has an ecstatic moment of rapture: "And then I caught sight of something. Ah ha! Glaucon, it looks as though there's a track here, so it seems that our quarry won't altogether escape us" (*Republic* 432b–d). It is shortly after that, though, that the interlocutors have to face the truth: before they can adequately say what justice is, they have to build a good "city" in speech, then apply and compare that paradigm to the soul, going back and forth dialectically (as if "rubbing fire-sticks together," 435a). They'll have to talk about the levels of reality (using two, now famous, analogies: the line and the cave), the ideal elementary and secondary education, and the cycle of political regimes before describing an after-death experience in which the justice of our souls is tested (the myth of Er, in Book X). In other words, to answer the seemingly simple question of what justice is, there are no shortcuts. This will be a *long* road: "Glaucon . . . we will never get a precise answer using our present methods of argument—although there is another longer and fuller road that does lead to such answers" (435d).

But all of this journeying along the road—that is, the attempt to find more and more basic realities—leads the interlocutor to something beyond "mere" goodness or even "mere" truth. At one point in Book VI, Socrates alludes to this "something beyond" before he realizes that his companions are spiritually and intellectually unprepared for the full vision:

Socrates: Well, then, [the guardian] must take the longer road and put as much effort into learning as into physical training, for otherwise . . . he will never reach the goal of the most important subject and the most appropriate one for him to learn.

Glaucon: Aren't these virtues, then, the most important things? . . . Is there anything even more important than justice and the other virtues we discussed?

Socrates: There is something more important. (*Republic* 504d)

There is something more important than virtue? Yes. And that "something more important" is "the form of the good" (505a). Socrates would like to tell his friends about it, but he realizes that they are not adequately prepared. At one point he tentatively explains, "Both knowledge and truth are beautiful things, but the good is other and more beautiful than they." Socrates's interlocutors babble rather stupidly: "This is an inconceivably beautiful thing you're talking about. . . . You surely don't think that a thing like that could be pleasure." Socrates replies, "Hush! Let's examine its image in more detail" (508e–509a).

Why can't they see it, too? Plato is not as explicit as we might wish, but, piecing together several passages from various dialogues, we can say that the reason has to do with the fact that Socrates's companions do not have the inner eye suited to seeing this aspect of ultimate reality. They are still using lower "knowledge faculties." The Good is "beyond being" and "beyond reason." It is not irrational, but it is prerational, we could say. It is beyond being, the cause of everything, and thus you have to climb the ladder of reality (beginning with moral and physical discipline, musical training, training in virtue, and rigorous intellectual training) before being ready to go beyond: "The good is not being, but superior to it in rank and power" (509c). You can't just jump to the end! You can't just go look at the Good, because you don't yet have the suitable internal equipment to see it.

Even if the dialogues lack external drama, they don't lack interior ambition. On the contrary, the vision of what it all aimed at sometimes left Plato breathless. Plato has to keep resorting to those wonderfully dramatic myths of the flight of the soul (the myth of the charioteer in *Phaedrus*), or the soul's ascent up a mystical ladder (Diotima's "ladder of love" in *Symposium*), or after-death experiences in which the soul will be tried (the myth of Er in the *Republic*). Plato's best dialogues follow similar patterns: they spiral upward to higher and higher and more and more abstract principles, which turn out to be foundational to the conversation. The interlocutors, led by Socrates, continue to ascend until Socrates can do nothing but reverently gesture at the "causeless" cause of all—that for which no more foundational reality can be found, that which, somehow, in some way, was not made, has always been, and cannot *not* be. It cannot have parts because, if it did, those parts could in turn be explained as simpler and more basic. It is not visible because, if it were, it would have a body; if it were bodily, then it would be changeable; and if it were changeable, then it would be corruptible. When the dialogue ascends to this point, Socrates just smiles and nods toward the Good in tones of hushed reverence. In this way, Platonic philosophy sublimates into prayer.

This happens in the *Symposium*. The prophetess Diotima explains the stages by which the mind ascends toward the apex of reality. It starts with a "falling in love" experience but goes far beyond that:

> After this he must think that the beauty of people's souls is more valuable than the beauty of their bodies. . . . [Then] our lover will be forced to gaze at the beauty of activities and laws and to see that all this is akin to itself. . . . After customs he must move on to various kinds of knowledge. . . . The lover [will be] turned to the great sea of beauty, and, gazing upon this, he gives birth to many gloriously beautiful ideas and theories, in unstinting love of wisdom, until, having grown and been strengthened there, he catches sight of such knowledge, and it is the knowledge of such beauty. (*Symposium* 210c–e)

Diotima mysteriously pauses and then, to make sure Socrates is listening, demands, "Try to pay attention to me." Although it is difficult to imagine anything more moving than gazing at the "sea of beauty" and "beautiful ideas," Diotima insists that there is a higher, more foundational reality:

> You see, the man who has been thus far guided in matters of Love, who has beheld beautiful things in the right order and correctly, is coming now to the goal of Loving: all of a sudden he will catch sight of something wonderfully beautiful in its nature; that, Socrates, is the reason for all his earlier labors. (210e)

In other words, the conversation begins in an attempt to explain the everyday experience of falling in love; but as the conversation unfolds, searching for deeper and deeper founding principles, they come at last to the ultimate explanatory principle, the cause-less cause of everything: exploring the highest possible realities has grounded the conversation on the lowest, most foundational level.

This is also the case in the dialogue *Phaedrus*, written around the same time. At one point Socrates delivers a speech arguing that the "falling in love" experience is so electric because it is a recol-lection of a kind of primordial memory of beauty itself. In love, we look into the eyes of the beloved and find that our entire soul "is suffused with a sense of warmth and starts to fill with tingles" (253e). We are struck by the beauty of the beloved's face "as if by a bolt of lightning" (254b). But this is because our "memory is carried back to the real nature of Beauty. . . . At the sight [the lover] is frightened, falls over backwards awestruck" (254b). The experience of beauty in love is shattering: "From the outlandish mix of these two feelings—pain and joy—comes anguish and helpless raving: in its madness the lover's soul cannot sleep at night or stay put by day; it rushes, yearning, wherever it expects to see the person who has that beauty" (251e). To explain this everyday experience, Socrates invents a wild myth, of a period before we were born, in which our souls would gather for grand processions with the gods and fly up into the heavens, and when we reached the "top" of heaven, we could gaze upon that which is "outside of heaven" (247e):

> The place beyond heaven—none of our earthly poets has ever sung or ever will sing its praises enough! Still, this is the way it is—risky as it may be, you see, I must attempt to speak the truth. . . . What is in this place is without color and without shape and without solidity, a being that really is what it is, the subject of all true knowledge, visible only to intelligence . . . and so [the soul] is delighted at last to be seeing what is real and watching what is true, feeding on all this and feeling wonderful, until the circular motion brings it around to where it started. (247d)

In Plato's imagination, this elaborate vision nourishes the inner soul and keeps it warm with delight for a whole year, until the next annual procession (248c). The experience is so moving that the closest analogy we have for "loveliness" itself is the first moment of "true love" when we are "struck by lightning" (254b). But even that is just a shadowy recollection of "things our soul saw when it was traveling with god" (249c).

We are now in a position to sum up some of these aspects of Plato's thought before concluding this chapter with a discussion of Plotinus. For Plato, the ultimate beauty can only be seen by a faculty that is higher than sense perception and higher even than the thinking skills of dialectic and mathematical reasoning. This is because the ultimate vision of what is really real—not in time, not in space, without color, and so forth—is so truly pure that we can only see it in the purest part of ourselves: "We gazed in rapture at sacred revealed objects that were perfect, and simple, and un-shakeable and blissful. That was the ultimate vision, and we saw it in pure light because we were pure ourselves" (*Phaedrus* 250c). That primordial moment of intellectual and spiritual rapture is a wordless gazing, a drinking in, a being moved in silent astonish-ment. This might explain why Plato insists on using the metaphor of "falling in love" to describe doing philosophy, a metaphor that does not come to mind for most of us when we think of philoso-phy professors in those corduroy jackets with elbow patches. But beauty is wounding, painful, so intensely real that it hurts and leaves you breathless, confused, anxious, and exhilarated. You go out of your mind when you first fall in love—you neglect your duties, seek out the beloved at all hours, make up stupid excuses to be near him or her. Plato calls this a "divine madness," superior to human self-control. Thus, only the "lover" can do philosophy! Why? Because only the lover is prepared for the consummation of philosophy, which is an act of ecstatic looking, excited wonder, an experience of confused and painful bliss.

In other words, for Plato, if we really want to understand what looking at the Good is like, we can never forget that "all of a sudden" moment, that split-second vision of the beloved when we are smitten, struck, wounded. This is the only way to experience Plato's Good. But even looking upon it for an age would not diminish that split-second quality. This "all-of-a-suddenness" never evaporates. To see the Good is always to look in a state of astonishment, for the first time, forever. And it is this experience that is foundational to my personality, the distant memory that is deeper to me than I am to myself, as Augustine would put it.

Plotinus and the Whispering Voice

The DNA of Plotinus's philosophy is made up of the intertwining ideas of ascent and descent found in Plato's *Phaedrus* and *Symposium*, even if Plotinus puts greater emphasis on beauty than love. For Plotinus, we are all born into this world under the conditions of metaphysical forgetfulness. To illustrate this he uses the almost Shakespearean thought experiment of a royal child, orphaned in infancy, who has noble blood in him but thinks he is a peasant. His inheritance is in the higher world—what Plato had called the "hyperouranian" plane—but he has forgotten that it even exists. And so, when we encounter traces of this higher world in an experience of beauty, we are stricken with a bizarre, violent surprise, because the experience of beauty carries with it more power than it seems like it ought to. Plotinus feels that it is his special duty to pry open these secret moments of beauty and show that they are more significant than you might suspect (*Enneads* V.1.1).

For Plotinus, then, we can imagine a kind of "long" soul that stretches down, below my rational consciousness, into the vital functions of my body but also stretches up above my rational consciousness.[8] On the one hand, my soul is constantly engaged in vital activities such as digestion and regulating my heartbeat; I can sometimes drag some of these activities into my consciousness, pay attention to them, and to some extent regulate them (like when I consciously control my breathing). But there are also activities my soul is engaged in at a level higher than my rational consciousness. In other words, there is a part of my soul—way down in there—that is actively connected to the One, the Good. And an encounter with beauty is the initial awakening to this deeper life.

At first it's too much to take in: "And what does this inner sight see? When it is just awakened it is not at all able to look at the brilliance before it" (*Enneads* I.6.9). But the more we tend to this experience of beauty, the more we sense and feel that there is depth stretching back beyond the horizons of our consciousness.[9]

But how do you move from the initial awakening to beauty to the fulfillment and culmination? As for Plato, the way up is the way down—or, better, the way within. And so Plotinus borrows all those dramatic myths—like Odysseus's homeward journey— and reapplies them to the drama of the soul.

> We shall put out to sea, as Odysseus did, from the witch Circe or Calypso—as the poet says (I think with a hidden meaning)—and was not content to stay though he had delights of the eyes and lived among much beauty of sense. Our country from which we came is there, our Father is there. How shall we travel to it, where is our way of escape? We cannot get there on foot; for our feet only carry us everywhere in this world, from one country to another. You must not get ready a carriage either, or a boat. Let all these things go, and do not look. Shut your eyes, and change to and wake another way of seeing, which everyone has but few use. (*Enneads* I.6.8)

Developing this way of seeing is a difficult process. It begins with an encounter with beauty, loosely defined. That could include art, music, or admiration for the character of a magnanimous, larger-than-life hero. When we have these moments—standing in front of a gigantic Rubens painting, with its sensuous surface; listening to Beethoven's "Ode to Joy" on New Year's Day; remembering old professors we deeply loved—we experience an inner "pull," a strange attraction that inexplicably makes us want to draw near or stand in their presence (*Enneads* I.6.4). And even deeper down, I intuit that this experience of beauty is related to my best self, the best version of me: "The soul, since by its nature what it is and is related to the higher kind of reality in the realm of being, when it sees something akin to it or a trace of its kindred reality, is delighted and thrilled and returns to itself and remembers itself and its own possessions" (I.6.2). The experience of ugliness is the exact opposite: repulsion, revulsion, a turning away (I.6.2).

There's another step. Being in the presence of such beauty doesn't just reverberate with the inner me but also makes me want to pull that best part up and out of me—to strip off all that is superfluous and useless and be the purest, cleanest version of me. By seeing beauty, I want to *be* beauty. When I see beauty, I have this sense that everything can change. I can start over. I can liberate the inner me. Plotinus, then, imagines a kind of dialectic in which I am shocked by beauty, inspired by it, reverberate with it (interiorly), and then resolve to impose more unity on my life (be less disordered) so that I slowly become like what I admire. Plotinus calls this working on your inner statue (*Enneads* I.6.9).

Over the course of time, as I polish the statue and reduce the difference between me and the external experience of beauty, a kind of inner light pools up within me, an intellectual generosity, a spiritual magnanimity. At this point, says Plotinus, I'm ready for the deep dive within. The first stripping was me detaching myself from addiction to the world, from feeling that I cannot be happy without sex or food or drink or excitement. But the second stripping is when I go to the top of my mind and draw my inner attention to beauty—but even then I have to realize that there's something beyond the rational. And so I come to the periphery of language and choose to walk over the edge into the darkness of the intellect. Plotinus occasionally refers to this as "stretching ourselves out with our soul into prayer to [the One], able in this way to pray alone to him alone" (*Enneads* V.1.6). Elsewhere he

talks about it as ascending a high set of stairs and entering the
darkness of the temple, where the One dwells alone:

> So we must ascend again to the good, which every soul desires. . . .
> The attainment of it is for those who go up to the higher world
> and are converted and strip off what we put on in our descent;
> (just as those who go up to the celebrations of sacred rites there
> are purifications, and strippings of the clothes they wore before,
> and going up naked) until, passing in the ascent all that is alien to
> the God, one sees with one's self alone That alone, simple, single
> and pure, from which all depends and to which all look and are and
> live and think. . . . If anyone sees it, what passion will he feel, what
> longing in his desire to be united with it, what a shock of delight!
> The man who has not seen it may desire it as good, but he who
> has seen it glories in its beauty and is full of wonder and delight,
> enduring a shock which causes no hurt, loving with true passion
> and piercing longing; he laughs at all other loves and despises
> what he thought beautiful before; it is like the experience of those
> who have met appearances of gods or spirits and do not any more
> appreciate as they did the beauty of other bodies. (*Enneads* I.6.7)

The One, beyond being and beyond reason, can be "sensed" or
"tasted" by some faculty in my soul too deep for words. We are left
in a silent dwelling-in-the-presence-of, not trying to answer any
problems or questions but just being there in quiet and "seeing."

3

The Inward Turn

What Augustine Learned from the Pagans

As the hart panteth after the water brooks, so panteth
 my soul after thee, O God.
My soul thirsteth for God, for the living God . . .
My tears have been my meat day and night.
                                        —Psalm 42:1–3

As we saw in the previous chapter, Plotinus was convinced
that we are born into the world as "orphans." Deep down
inside we have a fundamental orientation toward the
Good, but we have "forgotten our father" (*Enneads* V.1). Augustine believed this too, but with a very important difference. That
"One" or "Good," for Augustine, is a person who, unlike Plotinus's One, made us for himself and, to this end, continues to seek
us as we wander away from him in the barren desert (what Augustine calls the *regio dissimilitudinis*, the "region of unlikeness"—
everywhere God is not). Augustine most masterfully describes this
great drama in his *Confessions*.[1]

If for Plato we are awakened for the upward ascent through love, and for Plotinus through beauty, in the *Confessions* we find something new: the experience of weariness, soul fatigue, restlessness, and desolation can also nudge us to look higher.[2] Augustine, the man who spent the first three decades of his life doing little else but mastering the subtleties of language, leans into this feeling in the *Confessions*, summoning all the power of his literary art to create a portrait of the restlessness of our hearts, like some great Rembrandt of words. Again and again throughout this literary masterpiece, the late antique professor of rhetoric magically evokes this sense of heaviness of the soul. Sometimes we feel like we are pouring ourselves out uselessly: "I had spilt out my soul upon the sand" (*Conf.* IV.8, 62). Sometimes we feel like we are walking "through dark and slippery places," having gone out of ourselves in the search for the God of the heart (V.1, 95). Sometimes we feel like we've wasted the better part of our days in frenetic activity, which has left us interiorly depleted—indeed, cut and wounded in the soul. We feel fragmented, "torn asunder" (II.1, 25), or "tossed about and wasted and poured out and boiling over" (II.2, 25). At his most powerful, Augustine describes the soul in this "region of unlikeness" (VII.10, 129) wandering over the face of the earth, looking for a place to incarnate:

> I bore my soul all broken and bleeding and loathing to be borne by me; and I could find nowhere to set it down to rest. Not in shady groves, nor in mirth and music, nor in perfumed gardens, nor in formal banquets, nor in the delights of bedroom and bed, not in books nor in poetry could it find peace. I hated all things, hated the very light itself; and all that was not he was painful and wearisome, save only my tears. (*Conf.* IV.7, 61–62)

In this way, Augustine says, "I became a great enigma to myself and I was forever asking my soul why it was sad and why it disquieted me so sorely. And my soul knew not what to answer me" (IV.4, 59).

This restlessness is a fundamental concept in the *Confessions*. It's the unavoidable desolation that comes from committing the ur-sin of "cupidity," the primal sin of metaphysical forgetfulness—when we forget that creatures do not have their own beauty, but only a borrowed beauty (as Plotinus puts it). The technical Augustinian term for this is *cupiditas*, but at one point in the *Confessions* Augustine calls it, more colloquially, "immoderate inclination": "This life we live here below has its own attractiveness. . . . Yet in the enjoyment of all such things we commit sin if through immoderate inclination to them—for though they are good, they are of the lowest order of good—things higher and better are forgotten, even You, O Lord" (*Conf.* 2.5, 30). And if you live in this condition of having turned your back on God and forgotten him, you will be cranky and irritable and restless and angry and fragmented, bearing around with you your tired, lacerated soul. You seek fulfillment, constantly expecting that it is on the horizon, but it keeps moving farther away as you approach it. Like some modern artist or director, then, Augustine portrays a landscape of bleak desolation. In short, he is a master of describing the "Christ-haunted" self, which looks everywhere in this world for happiness but finds bitterness and disappointment in those things it put so much hope in obtaining. But, says Augustine, the extraordinary thing is that God has an active hand in the "mingling of bitter with sweet which brings us back to [Him] from the poison of pleasure that first drew us away from [Him]" (I.14, 16). Soul fatigue is one of the healing instruments of the God who is hunting us, even when we are lost.

As already noted, Plato and Plotinus's Good (or One) is awe-inspiring and beautiful and moving, but it is not personal. If you get a glimpse of Plato's "hyperouranian" plane, your soul will be filled with warmth for a whole year as you treasure the memory within. But the Good dwells abstractly, distantly, and in its infinite beauty is indifferent, beyond—indeed, ignorant of our existence, rather like Tuscany, which just dwells there in its beauty, unaware of whether you are actively photographing it or just remembering it now back home and far away.

But Augustine's God is different: he's a maker, sustainer, seeker, lover.[3] And because of this the Christian orator has to develop a new register of language, a kind of spellbinding, dreamlike, enchanting musical language no one had ever heard before. The brilliance of the *Confessions*, then, is that Augustine doesn't just *philosophize*; he speaks in the second-person singular to God, using the "you" form. And he creates a hypnotic spell by developing a style that expresses a sense of intimacy and presence. If Plotinus is like some musicologist you admire who makes you grow in admiration for your favorite composer by drawing your attention to the patterns and structures of a symphony, Augustine is the musician who performs it, who performs the presence of God:

> *Great art thou, O Lord, and greatly to be praised.* . . . And man desires to praise Thee. He is but a tiny part of all that Thou hast created. He bears about him his mortality, the evidence of his sinfulness, and the evidence that *Thou dost resist the proud:* yet this tiny part of all that Thou hast created desires to praise Thee. Thou dost so excite him that to praise Thee is his joy. For Thou hast made us for Thyself and our hearts are restless till they rest in Thee. (*Conf.* I.1, 3)[4]

This desire to address God as if he is present to me now, within, is what keeps Augustine's *Confessions* from being an ordinary autobiography. Indeed, if you read Augustine as if he is writing a simple tell-all, you'll be disappointed. He keeps interrupting himself with theological digressions or lyrical moments of praise, just as he's getting to the juicy bits you were hoping for! We have to understand the autobiographical elements, then, in the context of practicing the presence of God. Augustine's chief purpose is not to relate information.[5] Rather, he's hunting for the hidden God—hidden within his past life and within his memory.

Augustine doesn't imagine his spiritual growth as being on a line, moving from left to right, but rather as a series of onion layers in which new layers are added but earlier stages are still there within, so to speak (*Conf.* I.8). And so he walks back into his imagination, peeling back the layers of his development in order to find that God was there even if Augustine did not know it at the time. The most dramatic example of our ignorance of God, despite his presence, is infancy. Infants learn to speak without being taught how; they know how to suckle without prompting. The mother's breasts, he adds, fill with milk independently of her volition. Already, then, God is near to us as newborns before we even have the rational power to recognize it (I.6). And then Augustine tries to push God's presence even further back in time: "And before that again, O God of my joy? Was I anywhere? Was I anyone?" (I.6, 7). By walking all the way back into that time "buried in the darkness of the forgotten" (I.7, 9), well beyond the borders of his rational faculty, Augustine bumps into God, who was always already there: "Yet all the time You were more inward than the most inward place of my heart and loftier than the highest" (III.6, 44).

Infancy is an important theme for Augustine, in part because it is that liminal stage in which a human child finds herself wanting to interact with her parents—to express both her needs and her contentment—but does not yet have the words to express those desires. And so the infant struggles, cooing, flailing, doing her best to pour out her little heart. In other words, the infant is forced to try to tap into a language deeper than words. If I use a word you do not know, I can use a second word to clarify the first; and if you don't know *that* word, I can use a third to clarify the second. But if you know no words, how can I say anything to you at all? What the infant's parents intend must become clear by "a kind of natural language common to all races which consists in facial expressions, glances of the eye, gestures, and the tones by which the voice expresses the mind's state" (*Conf.* I.8, 10).

Fascinatingly, Augustine's interest in gesture and expression and wordless communication comes back later in the *Confessions* in a passage devoted to loss and love. Even in adult friendships we express things from our heart—we give "affection and receiv[e] it back, and shown by face, by voice, by the eyes, and a thousand other pleasing ways, kindl[e] a flame which fuse[s] our very souls and of many [make] us one" (*Conf.* IV.8, 63). For Augustine, the effortless language of love, of flashing eyes and beating heart, is the most proper language of prayer:

> But though I knew it not, You were listening. And when in silence I sought so vehemently, the voiceless contritions of my soul were strong cries to Your mercy. You knew what I was suffering and no man knew it. For how little it was that my tongue uttered of it in the ears even of my closest friends! Could they hear the tumult of my soul, for whose utterance no time or voice of mine would have been sufficient? Yet into Your hearing came all that I cried forth in the anguish of my heart, and my desire was in Your sight, and the light of my eyes shone not for me. (VII.7, 125)

Elsewhere Augustine says that the Word of God was made flesh so that "Your Wisdom, by which You created all things, might give suck to our souls' infancy" (VII.18, 133).

Putting all these strands together, this is an extraordinary modification of Plotinus's idea of "going within" to find God. We can go back and find God in our infancy and retroactively become present to the one whom we had ignored. Augustine uses all the powers of the "outer layer" of adulthood (his eloquence, his rationality) to return to the nearness and holy neediness of the inner infant. Indeed, the God who made us nourishes us in prayer too deep for words, prayer more akin to the infant's nursing. If it's somewhat startling for us to think about prayer in this way, we have to remember how shocked Augustine's contemporaries would have been![6] The *Confessions* are Augustine's attempt to walk back into the darkness of his own life, to discover with regret how God was there even though Augustine was absent from him, and then to utter a cry of "voiceless contrition" (VII.7, 125) from his "soul's depths" (VI.7, 104; VII.6, 122) to the one who had always already been there.

In light of this, any perceived borrowing from "the books of the Platonists" (as Augustine calls them in *Confessions* VII) will be complicated and multilayered. Without question, Augustine drew much from Plotinus, but he also reworked everything within a Christian context.[7] For example, Plotinus had used the Odyssean image of a man laboring to get home, as we have seen. Augustine borrows that image but reworks it within the context of Jesus's parable of the prodigal son (Luke 15:11–32): "To be darkened in heart is to be far from Thy face. It is not on our feet or by movement in space that we go from Thee or return to Thee: Thy prodigal son did not charter horses or chariots or ships, or fly with wings or journey on his two feet to that far country" (*Conf.* I.18, 19). Similarly, Augustine borrows the motif of ascent (compare the "ladder of love" or climbing the stairs of the temple in Plotinus, *Enneads* I.6). In Book VII, for example, Augustine describes his re-action to reading "the books of the Platonists" (*Conf.* VII.9, 126):

> Being admonished by all this to return to myself, I entered into my own depths, with You as guide; and I was able to do it because You were my helper. I entered, and with the eye of my soul, such as it was, I saw Your unchangeable Light shining over that same eye of my soul, over my mind. It was not the light of everyday that the eye of flesh can see, nor some greater light of the same order, such as might be if the brightness of our daily light should be seen shining with a more intense brightness and filling all things with its greatness. (VII.10, 128–29)

The books of the Platonists helped Augustine have a "break-through" moment in which, for the first time in his life, the "in-visible light" of God began to feel more real, seem more dense, and have more meaning than carnal realities had had throughout his life.[8] He was finally able to get a glimpse of that mysterious "invisible world" of intelligible Light, to *see* and *perceive* and *feel* it as something of weight and substance.[9] The Platonic authors had also taught Augustine that "the way up" was to "enter into

[his] own depths" and wake up a different faculty of knowing. Sometimes Augustine calls that mysterious faculty "the eye of the soul"—elsewhere, "the ear of the heart."[10] But all of it is heavily influenced by Platonism.[11] In another difficult but fascinating passage, Augustine gives us a few more tantalizing details about how this mystical vision came about:

> And I marvelled to find that at last I loved You and not some phantasm instead of You; yet I did not stably enjoy my God, but was ravished to You by Your beauty, yet soon was torn away from You again by my own weight. . . . I was altogether certain that Your *invisible things are clearly seen from the creation of the world, being understood by the things that are made:* so too are Your everlasting power and Your Godhead. I was now studying the ground of my admiration for the beauty of bodies, whether celestial or of earth. . . . Enquiring then what was the source of my judgment, when I did so judge I had discovered the immutable and true eternity of truth above my changing mind. Thus by stages I passed from bodies to the soul, . . . and from this to the soul's inner power . . . ; and from there I passed on to the reasoning power, to which is referred for judgment what is received from the body's senses. This too realised that it was mutable in me, and rose to its own understanding. It withdrew my thought from its habitual way, abstracting from the confused crowds of phantasms that it might find what light suffused it, when with utter certainty it cried aloud that the immutable was to be preferred to the mutable. . . . Thus in the thrust of a trembling glance my mind arrived at That Which Is. Then indeed I saw clearly Your *invisible things which are understood by the things that are made;* but I lacked the strength to hold my gaze fixed, and my weakness was beaten back again so that I returned to my old habits, bearing nothing with me but a memory of delight and a desire as for something of which I had caught the fragrance but which I had not yet the strength to eat. (*Conf.* VII.17, 132–33)

Again, here we can feel how Platonic Augustine is. He ascends to the divine by going within, and he does so by stages of ascent (think of the steps of the ladder of love). He moves from bodies to soul to the inner power of reasoning. But when he comes to the height of his contemplation, "in the thrust of a trembling glance" his mind arrives at That Which Is. And all of this reminds us of Plato ("All of a sudden he will catch sight of something wonderfully beautiful in its nature," *Symposium* 210e). In short, Augustine's contemplative trajectory moves from traces of God in the visible world to a perception of invisible things in themselves, as the two quotations from Romans 1:20 bookending this passage make clear.

But this comparison to the Platonic tradition also helps us see how Augustine's story departs from the Platonic account in important ways. First, whereas Plato posited the penultimate step of ascent to be "the great sea of beauty" where "gazing upon this, [one] gives birth to many gloriously beautiful ideas and theories," Augustine contemplates his own mind. In other words, Augustine is enamored not so much with some invisible realm of forms—which he doesn't seem to believe in—but with the very capacity of the human mind to find truth.[12] Later on in the *Confessions*, Augustine marvels at the astonishing capacity of his mind, not only for what it can store but also for what it can pass through, imaginatively, in an instant (X.8). In *On the Trinity*, Augustine famously develops an elaborate understanding of an inner trinity within us—that is, the infinitely subtle, psychological collaboration between our will, intellect, and memory, necessary in any use of our mind.[13] Thus, throughout his life, Augustine returned to the mind—its operations, its deep structure, and, even more abstrusely, its very ability to recognize the light of truth when it is encountered (such as in the "Eureka!" moment of solving a geometrical proposition). There is, then, an inner light, a light of the mind, that is analogous to the intelligible light enveloping God. Augustine's personality-based, psychologically driven inner exploration turns out to be more interior than Plotinus's!

The second important difference that emerges is that, for Augustine, the failure of the intellectual ascent can become the beginning of true prayer because it sparks the desire of our heart.

The soul's inability to launch itself all the way up to God can bring about the birth of longing, a new affective desire for God. Toward the end of his first description of the Platonic ascent, Augustine concludes,

> Thou art my God, I sigh to Thee, by day and by night. When first I knew Thee, Thou didst lift me up so that I might see that there was something to see, but that I was not yet the man to see it. And Thou didst beat back the weakness of my gaze, blazing upon me too strongly, and I was shaken with love and with dread. And I knew that I was far from Thee in the region of unlikeness, as if I heard Thy voice from on high: "I am the food of grown men: grow and you shall eat Me. And you shall not change Me into yourself as bodily food, but into Me you shall be changed." (*Conf.* VII.10, 129)

Plotinus, too, understood that in the first moment of revelation, the vision might be too bright for the soul, but Augustine understands that it is God who will provide him that nourishment to render him a spiritually grown man—a process of nourishment, as we have seen, that Augustine compares to nursing an infant. Here we are certainly no longer in the world of Plotinus. When Augustine's intellectual ascent falters and his soul flutters back down, he has to beg and plead. In other words, Augustine's intellectual ascent culminates in an affective, heartfelt prayer. When I cling to God like an infant to its mother, I am nourished in prayer. The intellectual ascent sublimates in the darkness of pure love.

Thus, Augustine's ascent has a new layer of "descent": it is not just that we have to go within but that we have to humble ourselves, stoop low, in imitation of Jesus Christ. This, of course, is where the Platonic ascent breaks down for Augustine. There's a big difference between the Platonist and the Christian. As Augustine puts it, "[I had begun] to discern the difference that there is between presumption and confession, between those who see what the goal is but do not see the way, and [those who see] the Way which leads to the country of blessedness, which we are meant not only to know but to dwell in" (*Conf.* VII.20, 136). The problem is that the Platonists don't know anything about *descent*. They know a lot about the lofty and the mighty and the strong and the ambitious. In Augustine's words, they "wear the high boots of their sublimer doctrine" (VII.9, 127). For this reason they have contempt for any talk about God's descent in the incarnation, about how that first principle or "One" became flesh—and thus they know nothing about confession, humility, and tears. In other words, they know nothing about infancy. But the God who nurses us in prayer was also once a baby, wailing, stretching forth his limbs, and trying to make himself understood: "The writings of the Platonists contain nothing of all this. Their pages show nothing of the face of that love, the tears of confession, Your sacrifice, an afflicted spirit, a contrite and humbled heart, the salvation of Your people. . . . And we hear no voice calling: *Come unto me, all you that labour*. They scorned to learn from Him, because He *is meek and humble of heart*." Augustine concludes, "It is one thing to see the land of peace from a wooded mountaintop, yet not find the way to it and struggle hopelessly far from the way . . . and quite another to hold to the way that leads there" (VII.21, 137).

For Augustine, then, the intellectual ascent was not good enough. It was merely the beginning of a new type of struggle—not just to know *that* God is or *where* he can be found but to "get good" at dwelling in his presence: "My desire now was not to be more sure of You but more steadfast in You" (*Conf.* VIII.1, 141). And so, after his conversion and in preparation for his entry into the church, Augustine begins to prayerfully make the Psalms his own words; praying through the Psalms is the medicine that his spirit needs to gain enough strength to dwell with God (VIII.4). The result of such prayerful discipleship is that he is able to proclaim, remarkably, that the things of the spirit have now become more real to him than the dubious goods of the world: "You began to make me feel Your love and to give *gladness in my heart*. . . . And I no longer wished any increase of earthly goods, in which a man wastes time and is wasted by time, since in the simplicity of the Eternal I had other *corn and wine and oil*" (IX.4, 170). Clearly, these are the effects of discipleship or, as Augustine prefers to put it, inner nourishment: in which God's Wisdom "might give suck" (VII.18, 133), in which the Christian might "breathe God in" (IX.7, 173) or let God's truth "flow in through the ears" (IX.6, 172), into the "hidden places of me" (VIII.11, 157) or *in intima mea* (VII.10, 128), because "You were more inward than the most inward place of my heart and loftier than the highest" (*tu autem eras interior intimo meo et superior summo meo*, III.6, 44).

Augustine never repudiated his "Platonic" vision, his vision of the blessed land from afar, but his Platonic vision had to find its perfection in another vision, one he enjoyed in the presence of his mother, Monica, at Ostia, after his entry into the Catholic Church and after an intense period of discipleship at Cassiciacum (see *Conf.* IX.10). I conclude this chapter with a close reading of that passage, because the Ostia scene is a literary masterpiece in which every detail matters.

By the time we get to this passage in *Confessions* IX.10, we have endured a long, emotionally exhausting narrative in which Augustine has told us all about his tempestuous struggle to come to God. But here, finally, we come to a little harbor in the story, a brief rest in his tale of restlessness. Indeed, Augustine describes the scene at Ostia as one of exceptional tranquility. Everything seems almost too good to be true, as if he and Monica have stepped unwittingly onto a movie set that has been prepared just for them. Indeed, it is only later that Augustine realizes that all this "came about, as I believe, by Your secret arrangement." The two travelers have nothing to do but wait for their imminent departure from the port city of Ostia, and as they rest from their land journey, waiting to go to sea, we have a sense of expectation, as though something is about to happen. Everything around Augustine and Monica is liminal, opening up onto something beyond itself: the window opens onto the garden; the land journey is about to give way to the journey at sea; the Tiber pours itself into the Tyrrhenian Sea. Within this symbolically charged environment, Augustine and Monica chatter away, but as they do they ascend by degrees to something beyond words, and it is part of the power of this passage that they enjoy such a stupendous vision in the midst of prosaic circumstances.

Although Augustine's description of their meandering conversation might at first seem haphazard, it is intelligible within the Platonic texts we have been reading as an ascending meditation—as Augustine says, "We climbed step by step up toward the selfsame [Augustine's name for God]" (*Conf.* IX.10, 178). The two begin by talking about the visible beauties of the world, the shining of sun and moon, before soaring still higher in their thought to a discussion of souls, until they come to "that region of richness unending, where you feed Israel forever with the food of truth: and there life is that Wisdom by which all things are made. . . . But this Wisdom itself is not made" (IX.10, 178). They move from the pleasure of the saints to the pleasure of bodies, and then to what extent the radiance of the lights of heaven gets at the arresting beauty of holiness. In other words, Augustine and Monica come to the conclusion that all the loveliness of the world is "not worthy of comparison with the pleasure of that eternal Light, not worthy even of mention" (IX.10, 179). Thus, in considering all the beautiful things the world has to offer, those things of the past, and present, and future, they conclude that all of them taken together are even then a dim shadow of all the pleasure, joy, and delight gathered into the "selfsame" God who "has ever been" and "shall be forever." But such a vision in this world is only transitory, and soon Augustine and Monica return "to the sound of [their] own tongue, in which a word has both beginning and ending" (IX.10, 179).

This tiered system of contemplation feels like an echo of Augustine's earlier, so-called Platonic ascent (*Conf.* VII.17).[14] Likewise, Augustine's Ostia ascent is, as we have come to expect, also an interior "descent": "And higher still we soared *within*" (IX.10, 179). Again, Augustine says that the vision came all of a sudden, in a single beat of the heart. And Augustine says that he and Monica stretched themselves out and in a moment of fleeting thought just managed to touch eternal wisdom.[15] Finally, Augustine describes their vision as being so intense that everything else afterward seemed trivial: "The world with all its delights seemed cheap to us in comparison with what we talked of" (IX.10, 130).[16]

In light of these parallels, we might ask this question: What *is* the difference between Augustine's Christian ascent at Ostia and his earlier Platonic ascent? One of the most interesting differences is the rich range of metaphors in his description of the Ostia ascent. The Platonic ascent of *Confessions* VII was a vision of light. In contrast, Augustine refers to the Ostia experience with a symphony of metaphors: it involved panting with the mouth of the heart, rising and soaring, a burning affection, attempting to "touch" God by coming to a region where God feeds Israel, and then leaving behind the "first fruits" of the spirit. Such touching, panting, longing, stretching out, reaching forth, tasting, and eating in Book IX is so different from the vision of the blessed land in Book VII, which is described exclusively in terms of light and vision. In particular, Augustine's insistence that, in the Ostia ascent, he and Monica "went beyond [their own souls] to come at last to that region of richness unending, where You feed Israel forever with the food of truth" (*Conf.* IX.10, 178), stands in sharp contrast to the conclusion to the Platonic ascent: "And I knew that I was far from Thee in the region of unlikeness, as if I heard Thy voice from on high: 'I am the food of grown men: grow and you shall eat Me. And you shall not change Me into yourself as bodily food, but into Me you shall be changed'" (VII.10, 129). Similarly, although the Platonic ascent involved perceiving a brilliant light too bright for the eye of his soul to take in, it did not involve the affections of the heart. In contrast, the Ostia ascent is full of the affections of the heart: stretching out, reaching forth, hungering, thirsting, and sighing, so that Augustine and Monica are ravished and absorbed and wrapped in "inward joys" (IX.10, 179).

As we have seen, this overflow of emotion into wordless gestures is how Augustine consistently describes his closest relationships. Earlier in Book IX, he wishes that unbelievers could be "somewhere close at hand—without my knowing that they were there—and could see my face and hear my words," and how his "emotions found expression in my eyes and in my voice" (*Conf.* IX.4, 168). When he is with his friend Alypius, struggling to convert, he comments, "My brow, cheeks, eyes, flush, the pitch of my voice, spoke my mind more powerfully than the words I uttered" (VIII.8, 153), just as friends, when welcoming other friends upon their return, greet one another with a warmth "proceeding from our hearts as we gave affection and received it back, and shown by face, by voice, by the eyes, and a thousand other pleasing ways, kindled a flame which fused our very souls and of many made us one" (IV.8, 63).

And it is this that makes the striking difference: Augustine's discovery of God occurs in the midst of an act of friendship with his mother. By loving I become more like love, which means I can better perceive Love itself. And, furthermore, Augustine can now begin to use the language of friendship and enjoyment with God, something unthinkable for Plotinus and his impersonal Good. Thus, for Augustine, the Christian life is one of continual ascent, vision, failure, and longing, but all this leads to the stirring of the heart with love for God. Beautiful and yet unsatisfying. Just a glance, not a gaze. Yet it is in our ardent affection for God that we begin to see his unveiled face. And while it is true that so many of Augustine's terms and ideas had already appeared in Plato and his followers, who described the One as the beginning and end of philosophy, at no point did they ever imagine that the Good could look back.

4

The Darkness of God

Dionysius the Areopagite, Gregory of Nyssa,
and Meister Eckhart

He made darkness his secret place; his pavilion round about him
were dark waters and thick clouds of the skies.

—Psalm 18:11

In the previous chapter we looked at some of Augustine's en-
dearing characteristics: he describes an intellectual ascent that
ends in the affection of the heart, and that fiery affection of
the heart pulls up from below what is deep down in the soul,
what is too deep for words. And because it is too deep for words,
Augustine can draw on a whole range of dazzling and sensuous
metaphors. Time and time again, Augustine tries to get at this
deep mode of knowing through some thought experiment. He
paradoxically describes a vision that begins to take on the over-
tones of tasting or even "feeling" (as in "warm embrace") God.

In this chapter, though, I want to talk about Christian writers
who are, we could say, "masters of darkness." That is, they do

not use the rich, positive, sensuous, bodily language of Augustine to show how far deep experiences of prayer surpass the ordinary experiences of everyday life; rather, they prefer the strong and acerbic metaphors of coldness and barrenness and desolation. These masters of darkness like to talk about the abyss and the desert and, above all, darkness instead of the taste and fragrance of God and the burning affection of the heart.

Are these ways of talking about the experience of God fundamentally at odds with one another? I don't think so. In fact, I think they are complementary. A God who is thought of only in terms of saturated sensation runs the risk of being only a God of enthusiasm and emotion; and a God who is thought of only in terms of darkness and desolation runs the risk of being only a remote principle or impersonal force, a Christian Nirvana. In the conclusion to this book, I will discuss John Ruusbroec and Nicholas of Cusa, two late medieval authors who had access to the full range of the mystical tradition up to their day, and I will speak admiringly about how they hold together in tension (1) what I am calling the positive tradition of affection and love (as found in Augustine, Bernard of Clairvaux, and Julian of Norwich) and (2) the negative tradition, which safeguards God's transcendence.

For now let's look at three brief portraits of perhaps the most challenging authors in the Christian mystical tradition. I won't attempt to make an apology for their views. Meister Eckhart tended to get himself in trouble because of his proclivity to blur the distinction between Christ and created human souls—that is, to explain what it means for God to be at the center of my soul in ways better suited to Plotinus than to Augustine.[1] I also have reservations about Eckhart's approach to creation and the natural world, even though his tendency to call for a radical detachment from all natural goods is consistent with other authors in the premodern world. We'll have to wait for modernity before we hear calls for a "world-affirming" mysticism. But here's the point: authors such as Gregory of Nyssa, Dionysius the Areopagite, and Meister Eckhart, although challenging and bold and on the razor's edge of orthodoxy, provide an irreplaceable service: they proclaim the radical transcendence of God with respect to the world. And, as there is no better way to drive that point home than by using the potent metaphors of darkness and desert, I'm going to let them have a voice, including Meister Eckhart. At the very least, they help keep us from superficially imagining God as part of this temporal and spatial world. You might sometimes prefer a scalpel, but that doesn't mean that a rock hammer is without its uses.

Knowing through Unknowing

Within the Christian tradition, "the mystic's mystic" is without a doubt the enigmatic Pseudo-Dionysius the Areopagite, who has a horrendously frightening name that requires immediate explanation. In Acts 17, the apostle Paul delivers a famous speech in Athens on Mars Hill, known in Greek as the *Areios Pagos* or Areopagus ("the hill of Ares"). Paul builds a rhetorical case for Christianity on the basis of an inscription he sees on an altar, one dedicated to "the unknown god," which for the Athenians seemingly functioned as a kind of safety mechanism to make sure they didn't leave out any deity important for their well-being. Paul, though, seizes on the inscription's ambiguity and takes the opportunity to proclaim to the Athenians *who* that unknown God is, claiming that he is actually the God of Christianity, who, previously hidden and unknown, now wishes to make himself known even to Greek-speaking pagans through the person of Jesus, lately incarnate. The Athenians enjoy Paul's speech because, as the heirs of Socrates, they delight in all tour de force rhetorical performances.[2] They just are not persuaded by it, except for two people, one of whom is named Dionysius. Scripture says only this: "And when they heard of the resurrection of the dead, some mocked: and others said, We will hear thee again of this matter. So Paul departed from among them. Howbeit certain men clave unto him, and believed: among the which was

Dionysius the Areopagite, and a woman named Damaris, and others with them" (Acts 17:32–34).

We know nothing more about this mysterious convert Dionysius who responded to the call of the gospel on the Areopagus. However, a sixth-century, Greek-speaking Byzantine theologian (heavily influenced by Greek Neoplatonism, which was enjoying its last revival in the Platonic Academy under the leadership of a man named Proclus) adopted as a pen name—or, better, as a fictional literary identity—the name of Dionysius, and he wrote as if he were indeed that disciple who had been tutored in private by Paul. Paul himself had made some suggestive remarks in 2 Corinthians 12 about some sort of ecstatic experience—but then, tantalizingly, he refused to explain it. This is where the writer known as Dionysius comes in. He built his literary identity on being the one who knew about that experience and how others might attain that vision. Thus, we have all the needed ingredients to ensure the extraordinary success of Dionysius the Areopagite's writings in both the Greek and the Latin Middle Ages: an alleged disciple of the great St. Paul who had unique behind-the-scenes access to Paul's mystical vision and was personally given a "method" to help the minds of those already advanced in spirituality achieve the same heights. And so, just one century after Dionysius's writings were composed (sometime around AD 500), they were already being read as though they had actually been penned by a writer of the apostolic generation. In this way, this sixth-century Platonizing Christian became the single greatest stimulus to mysticism until his identity was "exposed" in the Renaissance. That's why he is today called "*Pseudo*-Dionysius the Areopagite."

For our purposes, it doesn't really matter *why* Pseudo-Dionysius laid claim to such apostolic authority. Was it a deliberate deception to gain authority? Was it, as Hans Urs von Balthasar suggested, a mark of intellectual humility (as if to say, "Everything I have come to know is just an exposition of the teaching of Paul")? My own feeling is that the pseudonymity of Dionysius is motivated by his desire to conduct a literary thought experiment in which he brings

his Greek learning to bear on Scripture. In other words, I don't
see any fraudulent attempt to deceive, although the intentions of
the author do not make much difference for our present purposes.

More than anything else, this sixth-century Byzantine writer
was interested in the God who rests in "the brilliant darkness of
a hidden silence" (Pseudo-Dionysius, *MT* 1).[3] In this way he was
a child of his age, the inheritor of a centuries-long, rich tradition
of negative theology. Not just the pagan Platonists but the entire
age, so unlike modernity, was tuned in to God's infinite transcendence. In addition to the so-called Middle Platonists and Neopla-
tonists (like Albinus and Plotinus), Jewish philosophers such as
Philo were particularly sensitive about making sure God was not
mingled with his creatures. And so, a famous Greek particle (the
so-called alpha privative, an alpha attached to the beginning of
an adjective, negating the word) began to pop up everywhere. "As
the pre-Christian passed into the Christian era, . . . the negative
adjectives thus formed show 'a tendency to magnify the mystery
of God.'"[4] God was *a-theatos* (*not* visible to the eyes); *a-choretos*
(*not* located within space); *a-genetos* (*not* born); *an-endees* (*not*
needy); *a-perigraphos* (incapable of being described in words); *a-
perinoetos* (unable for us to get a concept around); *a-nonomastos*
(unable to be named); *a-kataleptos* (*not* comprehensible).

Such words of negation make their way into Paul, who praises
God as *a-oratos* (*not* able to be seen, Rom. 1:20; compare Col. 1:15);
a-rhetos (*not* able to be spoken, 2 Cor. 12:4); *an-ekdiegetos* (incapable of being properly explained, 2 Cor. 9:15); *an-exereunetos*
(*not* able to be searched out, Rom. 11:33); *a-prositos* (*not* nearby,
1 Tim. 6:16).[5] In the second century, Justin Martyr, a Christian
apologist, took advantage of this understanding of the infinite
remoteness of God and used it against the pagans: "Justin Martyr,
the first among the Fathers to emphasize divine ineffability, says
anyone who would want to name the inexpressible God suffers
from an incurable madness."[6] But throughout the early Christian
centuries, in which authors were sensitive to the "darkness" of
God, delighting in it and drinking it in like the blackness of the

night, there was no Christian who had yet formulated a method or path through such negativity—a path that would come to be known as the *via negativa*. This is exactly what Dionysius did, equipped with his Platonic learning, and this is how he secured for himself the role of "the mystic's mystic."

Dionysius wrote several medieval "bestsellers," including two treatises on how the hierarchy of the angels mirrored the ecclesiastical hierarchy, *The Celestial Hierarchy* and *The Ecclesiastical Hierarchy* (so very fitting in imperial Byzantium), and another treatise in which he scours all the names and characteristics attributed to God in the Bible (and venerable ancient sources) and asks in what sense they either appropriately capture the essence of God or fail to get at his essence (*The Divine Names*).[7] Thus, before we look at Dionysius's short Pauline-esque "epistle" on mysticism addressed to "Timothy," I will devote some words to describing his "theophanic" vision of the universe.

Much of Dionysius's thinking is rooted in metaphors of flowing down from a lofty source.[8] Imagine a series of waterfalls tumbling down from a height and then flowing into a mountain valley. If you, coming from below, were to follow those various streams all the way up to the top, where the snows slowly release their waters when they melt in late spring, you would have something analogous to how Dionysius feels about the universe. It all flows forth from its Cause, God, whose ecstatic goodness flows forth in the joy of making the visible world.[9] For Dionysius, every drop of water, no matter how far it has moved away from its remote mountain source, is related to its Cause (even if it differs in "state," such as the liquid versus solid precipitation in my example). In this way it carries with it a vestige of where it came from. It is a kind of distant reflection of its origin: "Everything, and every part of everything, participates in the One, and on the existence of the One everything depends for its existence."[10]

But to this moving vision Dionysius adds another layer: this providential Cause is also a loving God, one who is not just the source of creation (as was true for Plotinus) but one who remains surprisingly exuberant about creation. God is ecstatic about us. In general, when we are pulled out of ourselves in "yearning," we feel like we belong "not to self but to the beloved"—but Dionysius is so bold as to say that the Creator experiences the same thing with respect to creation: "We must dare to add this as being no less true; that the Source of all things Himself, in His wonderful and good love for all things, through the excess of His loving goodness, is carried outside Himself, in his providential care for all that is, so enchanted is He in goodness and love and longing. Removed from His position above all and beyond all He descends to be in all according to an ecstatic and transcendent power which is yet inseparable from Himself."[11] We have, then, not just a flowing down from the mountains into the valley but a sustaining, providential care, as if in the waters there is a counterforce at work, trying to turn the waters back upward toward their source. For this reason Dionysius imagines the world not just as a flow of liquid but as a flow that nourishes, uplifts, and even "inebriates," like an extravagant river that is simultaneously made up of milk, wine, water, and honey.[12]

This divine love (or *eros*) is at the heart of Dionysius's theophanic vision of the cosmos; that is, creation not only flows from its source in the goodness of God but, when awakened, can become a symbol pointing our minds upward. The universe is a kind of dazzling assembly of mirrors—or, maybe better, stained-glass windows, some more and some less transparent—and part of the human (and angelic!) drama is to render this world as brilliant as possible:

> In my opinion a hierarchy is a sacred order, a state of understanding and an activity approximating as closely as possible to the divine. And it is uplifted to the imitation of God in proportion to the enlightenments divinely given to it. The beauty of God—so simple, so good, so much the source of perfection—is completely uncontaminated by dissimilarity. It reaches out to grant every being, according to merit, a share of light and then through a divine sacrament, in harmony and in peace, it bestows on each of those being perfected its own form.[13]

The twentieth-century Swiss theologian Hans Urs von Balthasar sums up this *theophanic* aspect of Dionysius's thought: "Denys [Dionysius] contemplates the divine symbols in creation and the Church with an aesthetic delight. Things are not simply the occasion for his seeing God; rather, he sees God in things. Colours, shapes, essences and properties are for him immediate theophanies. . . . One can only with difficulty resist the temptation to quote profusely the theological portrayals by this poet of water, wind and clouds, and particularly of the fragrance of God."[14] This is the positive aspect of Dionysius. But the Syrian author also has a negative (or apophatic) teaching.

Even though each creature is related to its distant Cause and thus can manifest something of God when illuminated, it is also true that, however similar the creature is to God, there is still an infinite dissimilarity. So Dionysius draws an extraordinary conclusion: our knowledge can get in the way of our ability to perceive God. Rather, he says, we have to carve away our knowledge until we get to that inner essence that is "beyond" knowing. We have to "deny all things," he says with infinite paradox, "so that we may unhiddenly know that unknowing which itself is hidden from all those possessed of knowing amid all beings." If we do this we will "see above being that darkness concealed from all the light among beings" (*MT* 2).

Imagine an orchestra playing a symphony, bringing into being the "pure" score of some brilliant composer. The music, as it is played, gives us some insight into the composer's creativity, but at the same time we have to admit that there is so much more to the composer's genius than is made manifest in a single piece of music or even in a whole oeuvre. The symphony both reveals and conceals the genius of the composer, a genius that cannot be reduced to any single composition. Every note, we could go so far as to say, both tells us something of the composer and at the same time totally fails to reveal the composer's essence. Analogously, says Dionysius, we can make the paradoxical claim that God is everything in everything but is not identical with those things:

"Providence occurs everywhere. It contains everything and, at the same time, it is something in something, but in a transcending way; in no way is it nothing in nothing. For it quite surpasses everything."[15]

What does this mean? And how do you go about this "looking beyond"? After you have used the positive "symbols" to climb your way back up to the top of creation, you have to then "negate" them in order to ascend even higher. Dionysius believes that there are many things you can (sort of) say about God through what he calls affirmative (or kataphatic) theology. You can say that God is one as well as triune. You can talk about his "Fatherhood" and "Sonship" and of the "Spirit." You can even peruse Scripture (and the ancient philosophers renowned for their piety) and find other fascinating names and "symbols." God can rightly be described as "good, existent, life, wisdom, power, and whatever other things pertain to the conceptual names for God" (*MT* 3). And again, because God is the cause of everything, all things have something that, however remotely, hints, gestures, and gesticulates toward God. In a way, the whole world is a series of potential "names" that tell us something, however slight, about God.

It is for this reason that Dionysius has a particular penchant for "dissimilar symbols"—that is, weirdly difficult metaphors (Dionysius mentions strange references to divine "drunkenness"): by using them, we are not tempted to think that we are getting at the essence of God. We are so puzzled by what we hear that we know we are dealing with a metaphor. The difficulty is that even lofty terms such as "good" and "being" are metaphorical. Picking up on language found in Plato, Plotinus, and Proclus, Dionysius says that because the One is "beyond intellect" and "beyond being," all language fails to lay claim to his essence. The One (or, here, God) is "the Cause of all" and thus "is above all" (*MT* 4). So we have to be particularly on guard against high and lofty names. We have to test those lofty attributes, put them on trial, and pay attention as we watch them also fail: "The fact is that the more we take flight upward, the more our words are confined to the ideas we are capable of forming; so that now as we plunge into that darkness which is beyond intellect, we shall find ourselves not simply running short of words but actually speechless and unknowing. . . . My argument now rises from what is below up to the transcendent, and the more it climbs, the more language falters, and when it has passed up and beyond the ascent, it will turn silent completely, since it will finally be at one with him who is indescribable" (*MT* 3). We have to talk ourselves into speechlessness.

Precisely because this experience of moving from concepts to God is a process of moving beyond ideas to the living, burning fullness of the divine, Dionysius employs a broad range of daring metaphors: going from the "right answer" to the fullness of reality is a "plunging" (like a diver holding his breath before he leaps from a precipitous cliff) or a "soaring" or "climbing" up into zones where the air is thin and clean. The Word of God is "on a plane above all [word, act of understanding], and it is made manifest only to those who travel through foul and fair, who pass beyond the summit of every holy ascent, who leave behind them every divine light, every voice, every word from heaven, and who plunge into the darkness where . . . there dwells the One who is beyond all things" (*MT* 1). Later, Dionysius warns us not to confuse "walking the heights of those holy places to which the mind at least can rise" with knowing God himself. Like Moses, you must go even higher: "But then he [Moses] breaks free of them, away from what sees and is seen, and he plunges into the truly mysterious darkness of unknowing. Here, renouncing all that the mind may conceive, wrapped entirely in the intangible and the invisible, he belongs completely to him who is beyond everything. Here, being neither oneself nor someone else, one is supremely united to the completely unknown by an inactivity of all knowledge, and knows beyond the mind by knowing nothing" (*MT* 1). Elsewhere, Dionysius also uses a potent artistic metaphor, that of a sculptor who chips away at the surface until what is left is nothing but the inner core: "We would be like sculptors who set out to carve a statue. They remove every obstacle to the pure

view of the hidden image, and simply by this act of clearing aside
they show up the beauty which is hidden" (*MT* 2). Even good and
correct divine attributes have to be carved away!

Why do we have to walk, climb, soar, or carve away, according
to this way of denial? Because we don't want a mere concept to get
in our way! Because the light of our intellect can eclipse the brilliant darkness of God. All of our concepts come from creatures,
which are caused—which have their being on loan, as it were. In
contrast, Dionysius says (borrowing an extraordinary phrase from
Plato), God is "beyond being": he cannot *not* "be." Nor can he
be "thought" because, for a good Greek, thought is a generalized
concept drawn from the beings we find around us. For this reason
God is "beyond all being and knowledge" (*MT* 1).[16]

It is this dual focus, God as Cause but God as distinct from
beings, that gives rise to Dionysius's method. We have to affirm
everything and then deny everything: "What has actually to be
said about the Cause of everything is this. Since it is the Cause
of all beings, we should posit and ascribe to it all the affirmations we make in regard to beings, and, more appropriately, we
should negate all these affirmations, since it surpasses all being."
Clearly, such a "negation" is not saying that God is the opposite
of being, goodness, or life but rather that he is too expansive for
our ordinary, positive language to be trustworthy: "We should
not conclude that the negations are simply the opposites of the
affirmations, but rather that the cause of all is considerably prior
to this, beyond privations, beyond every denial, beyond every assertion" (*MT* 1). Thus, we have to employ an *askesis* of the mind, a
discipline of our words. We must have the ability to practice a holy
silence. And it is exactly this *askesis* of the mind that Dionysius
"performs" for us at the end of his short epistle:

> The Cause of all is above all and is not inexistent, lifeless, speech-
> less, mindless. It is not a material body, and hence has neither shape
> nor form, quality, quantity, or weight. . . . Again, as we climb higher
> we say this. It is not soul or mind, nor does it possess imagination,

conviction, speech, or understanding. . . . It cannot be spoken of and it cannot be grasped by understanding. . . . There is no speaking of it, nor name nor knowledge of it. Darkness and light, error and truth—it is none of these. It is beyond assertion and denial. We make assertions and denials of what is next to it, but never of it, for it is both beyond every assertion . . . and, by virtue of its preeminently simple and absolute nature, free of every limitation, beyond every limitation; it is also beyond every denial. (*MT* 4–5)

With Moses in the Enveloping Darkness

Dionysius was not the only Greek "master of darkness" in the ancient world. Two centuries before him Gregory of Nyssa explored what we could call the subjective dimension of the doctrine of God's hiddenness. Gregory (ca. AD 335–395) was the younger brother of Basil of Caesarea—Gregory, Basil, and Gregory of Nazianzus are referred to as the Cappadocian Fathers.[17] They took part in one of the first great golden ages of Christian theology. In Gregory of Nyssa's *Life of Moses* we find a fruitful juxtaposition of Greek learning and scriptural study.

Gregory's retelling of and commentary on Exodus begins with a brotherly epistle in which Gregory tells the recipient that he is cheering him on to run even faster in the spiritual race, like some fanatical fan at an ancient horse race yelling for his favorite charioteer. Indeed, the goal—the "turning post" in the race of the Christian life—that Gregory proposes for his spiritual brother is nothing less than "the perfect life" (*Life* I.2, 29).[18] Gregory immediately qualifies what he means by "the perfect life": it is not just a life of possessing virtues (*Life* I.6) but something more, something greater, something on which even the virtues must be founded. In fact, he says shockingly, "it is . . . impossible for those who pursue the life of virtue to attain perfection" (*Life* I.6, 31). Those seeking virtue—or those seeking some sort of mastery or self-control, a state of "not sinning"—miss both the point and the real secret of the Christian life. God is limitless, says Gregory, and thus we have to stretch infinitely out into him. The Christian life is not about locking down but about "limitless desire": "Since this good has no limit, the participant's desire itself necessarily has no stopping place but stretches out with the limitless" (*Life* I.7, 31). But what does all this mean? And how do you get to this point of infinite desire? Gregory proposes for his brother's consideration a spiritual reading of the life of Moses.

In Book I, Gregory gives an action-packed summary of the life of Moses, turning Moses into some kind of ancient superhero, a man of strength and feats and accomplishments. Moses slays an Egyptian, crosses the Red Sea, follows the cloud, crafts a bronze serpent, strikes a rock to produce water, and so on. But already in this section, which purports to be just a quick (albeit "amplified") narrative summary, we can see that Gregory is particularly interested in two events in the life of Moses: the epiphany of the burning bush and Moses's ascent of the mountain where he encounters God, receives the law, and is given a vision of the tabernacle while his worldly and carnal countrymen tremble at the foot of the mountain (*Life* I.1–74).

In Book II, Gregory revisits the narrative events laid out in Book I, now proposing spiritual, allegorical, and typological interpretations; that is, some events in Moses's life point forward to events in the New Testament (to take one example, for Gregory, the fact that the bush is not consumed by fire is a clear "type" of the perpetual virginity of Mary, who was not "consumed" when she was touched by God [*Life* II.21, 59]). The fact that the Israelites are only given enough food to suffice for a single day represents that the "insatiable greed of those always hoarding surplus is turned into worms. Everything beyond what they need encompassed by this covetous desire becomes on the next day—that is in the future life—a worm to the person who hoards it" (II.143, 89). Moses took off his sandals in God's presence, so we should take off the sandals of our soul—that is, put aside worldly-mindedness (II.23).

But what Gregory is interested in more than anything else is the vertical ascent beyond the high mountain plane of "mere" virtue:

"The Scripture leads our understanding upward to the higher levels of virtue. For the man [Moses] who received strength from the
food and showed his power in fighting with his enemies and was
the victor over his opponents is then led to the ineffable knowledge
of God" (*Life* II.152, 91). In fact, all other achievements of virtue
and discipline are merely preparatory for this ascent. Because
Moses has looked to the cloud for guidance (allegorically: followed the law and achieved virtue), has been purified by crossing
the Red Sea, has tasted the bitter waters that later are found to be
sweet (that is, "the life removed far from pleasures"), has received
heavenly bread, and has stretched out his arms to win victories
(that is, foreshadowed how the law anticipates the cross), he is
now ready for "contemplation of the transcendent nature." Moses
has sought absolute and total purity: "The one person who would
approach the contemplation of Being must be pure in all things so
as to be pure in soul and body, washed stainless of every spot . . .
in order that he might appear pure to the One who sees what is
hidden" (II.153, 92). Then we are ready for the mountain, "steep
indeed and difficult to climb—the majority of people scarcely
reach its base" (II.158, 93). To do this, Moses must deprive himself
of all reliance on the senses and ordinary rational procedures, for
"the contemplation of God is not effected by sight and hearing,
nor is it comprehended by any of the customary perceptions of
the mind" (II.157, 93). We're now in familiar Platonic territory.

It is here that Gregory begins to approach the most mysterious
part of his teaching, on entering the "darkness" at the top of the
mountain. Gregory points out that earlier manifestations of the
presence of God had come in the form of light, representing divine
illumination. But when we come to the scene in which Moses approaches Sinai, we find darkness:

> Let us not think that this is at variance with the sequence of things
> we have contemplated spiritually. Scripture teaches by this that
> religious knowledge comes at first to those who receive it as light.
> Therefore what is perceived to be contrary to religion is darkness,

and the escape from darkness comes about when one participates in light. But as the mind progresses and, through an ever greater and more perfect diligence, comes to apprehend reality, as it approaches more nearly to contemplation, it sees more clearly what of the divine nature is uncontemplated.

For leaving behind everything that is observed, not only what sense comprehends but also what the intelligence thinks it sees, it keeps on penetrating deeper until by the intelligence's yearning for understanding it gains access to the invisible and the incomprehensible, and there it sees God. This is the true knowledge of what is sought; this is the seeing that consists in not seeing, because that which is sought transcends all knowledge, being separated on all sides by incomprehensibility as by a kind of darkness. Wherefore John the sublime, who penetrated into the luminous darkness, says, 'No one has ever seen God,' thus asserting that knowledge of the divine essence is unattainable not only by men but also by every intelligent creature. (*Life* II.162–63, 95)

This brings us to the heart of what is most distinctive and extraordinary in Gregory's treatise, his doctrine of "eternal progress" (*epektasis*, a kind of "hyperecstasy" or "ecstasy beyond the ecstatic"). Gregory teaches that within the vision of God there is an ever-increasing vision, a kind of eternal "falling inward" into God, in which the mind moves from "glory to glory," always upward, from height to height, and there is no limit to how many peaks the mind may continue to scale: "This truly is the vision of God: never to be satisfied in the desire to see him. But one must always, by looking at what he can see, rekindle his desire to see more. Thus, no limit would interrupt growth in the ascent to God, since no limit to the Good can be found nor is the increasing of desire for the Good brought to an end because it is satisfied" (*Life* II.239, 116).

Gregory sets up this description of contemplation by focusing on the tension between two scriptural verses: (1) the one in which the Lord speaks to Moses "face to face, as a man speaketh unto his friend" (Exod. 33:11); and (2) the passage that immediately follows, which says that Moses is only allowed to see God's back.[19] For Gregory, all thought of spatial dimensions in relation to God ("front" and "back") have to be discarded immediately (II.221–22). Things that dwell in space are composite; composite things, made up of pieces, can come "unglued" and thus are not eternal. Clearly, then, God does not possess a "face" and a "back" in this sense. We have to push on and go deeper into the spiritual meaning of the Scriptures (II.219). If God is "beyond being," and if we cannot confuse knowing him with knowing metaphysical realities, then our knowing of him is potentially infinite. Indeed, in every encounter with God, the horizon moves farther back. Imagine standing on the shore of an ocean and straining your eyes to look out toward the horizon. You know that if you were to get into a boat and sail to that point, the horizon would be farther back still. Gregory imagines God to be like a sea without end. The horizon of the ocean is always moving back. And this is Gregory's famous doctrine of *epektasis:* "The doctrine that every arrival in the process of spiritual growth is but a new point of departure, and continued progress is the law of spiritual life even in the next world, in the beatific vision."[20]

This is where Gregory's thought takes on a dizzying tone. Although Moses had a whole lifetime of achievements, feats, and accomplishments, he was still restless for more:

> He made camps under the cloud. He quenched thirst with the rock. He produced bread from heaven. By stretching out his hands, he overcame the foreigner. He heard the trumpet. He entered the darkness. . . . He shone with glory. And although lifted up through such lofty experiences, he is still unsatisfied in his desire for more. He still thirsts for that with which he constantly filled himself to capacity, and he asks to attain as if he had never partaken, beseeching God to appear to him, not according to his capacity to partake, but according to God's true being. (*Life* II.229–30, 114)

The ardent soul "loves what is beautiful," is drawn "to what is beyond," and "longs to be filled with the very stamp of the archetype" to "enjoy the Beauty not in mirrors and reflections, but face to face" (II.231–32, 114–15). This is because the more effort a soul makes in its pursuit of virtue, the greater capacity it has for love. And that greater capacity for love means that the soul can see more of God. But what it sees is so inspiring that it wants to push on in the life of virtue, which expands its capacity to love, which increases its capacity to see, which fills it with greater desire to be virtuous, and so on, in a virtuous cycle of "eternal progress." God cannot "satisfy" the desire of the soul, because he always has more beauty in reserve, so to speak, which remains on the periphery of the soul's ability to see. But his desire is to give it all, even if we can only take it in stages.

And so our subjective experience of encountering God is one of "falling" precipitously into him or, to use a metaphor from Gregory, of stepping on the first rung of a ladder, then on the next one, then another higher up, and then another, only to realize that the ladder is infinitely high (*Life* II.227). We can also imagine this ascent as taking flight: "Made to desire and not to abandon the transcendent height by the things already attained, [the soul] makes its way upward without ceasing, ever through its prior accomplishments renewing its intensity for the flight. Activity directed toward virtue causes its capacity to grow through exertion; this kind of activity alone does not slacken its intensity by the effort, but increases it" (II.226, 113). This leads to a paradoxical "movement in stillness" in which one stands and ascends simultaneously, a kind of flight or diving into depth more violent and dizzying than any physical motion, all the while remaining completely still (II.243). Thus, we have to be careful not to enclose God within our minds, either in terms of imagining that the "perfect" life consists in mere virtue, or in our too narrow imagining of the infinite, churning sea of God's joy: "It is not in the nature of what is unenclosed to be grasped. But every desire for the Good which is attracted to that ascent constantly expands as one progresses in pressing on to the Good" (II.238, 116).

If we could get a glimpse of this vision—get a glimpse of God, look upon him "face to face" and have a taste of what it means to be "the friend of God" (*Life* II.319), to be known and seen by God (II.320), to have "bright, shining eyes that don't grow dim with age" (II.318)—then things in this life such as the allure of the flesh (II.312, 316) and the ambition for titles and promotions (II.309) would have no sway over us. We would just smile at them, as though viewing them from a great height: "[Moses] stood above human honor and beyond royal dignity, considering it to be stronger and more royal to keep watch for virtue and to be beautified with its adornment than to be a spearman and to wear royal adornment. . . . He who preferred to live by what flowed from above no longer tasted earthly food" (II.313, 133–34). The good that flows from above is "unenclosed," an abyss of joy that makes every measured, proportional, and "closed" creaturely good pallid in its light. We have to "protect" God from our images of him because to "enclose" God is spiritual death: "He who thinks God is something to be known does not have life, because he has turned from true Being to what he considers by sense perception to have being" (II.234, 115). Rather, we have to be motivated by a sacred restlessness, to be bold, to go up the mountain, to hunger to "enjoy the Beauty not in mirrors and reflections, but face to face" (II.232, 114–15).

Meister Eckhart: God's Rock Hammer

When Meister Eckhart (ca. 1260–1328) had to defend himself against charges of heresy at the end of his life, he based his case on two arguments. First, it was impossible for him to be a heretic, he declared, because a heretic is one who stubbornly clings to doctrine that has been judged an error: "I am able to be in error, but I cannot be a heretic, for the first belongs to the intellect, the second to the will."[21] Eckhart promised to renounce anything judged to be in error. His second argument was that everything he preached was based on the principle of "insofar as"—that is, on the principle of likeness and similarity—or as he put it in one sermon, "I would like now to focus on the little word *quasi* which means 'as.' . . . This is what I focus on in all my sermons" (Sermon 9).[22] In other words, the Parisian professor, dialectician, and master of theology was keenly aware of what Dionysius and Gregory of Nyssa had been concerned with: the limitations of language when describing the cause of being. When we talk about God, we always have to use "as if." For Eckhart, God was *puritas essendi* ("purity of being"), the "being of being," not like things themselves but that without which they could not be. To get at *that* requires something more than language, something higher than language. Or rather, language exists in order to help us climb all the way up to the top before we have to leave it behind.

As a Dominican, Eckhart preached in the everyday language of merchants, knights, men of business, housewives, craftsmen, and servants (imagine the ragtag group of tradesmen and petty nobles in *The Canterbury Tales*, just in Cologne or Strasbourg). Over the course of his career, when he was not serving as an academic in Paris, he oversaw the Dominican houses in Saxony and served as the representative of the Master General of the Dominican order in Strasbourg; thus, he had many opportunities to develop a way of speaking that could move a nonclerical, uneducated, and often illiterate audience, even in the midst of their practically minded bustle. In his German-language sermons, Eckhart tries to do something extraordinary: drag all of his learning into a language that, at the time, lacked the infinitely subtle precision and terminology of centuries of Scholastic refinement. And in this effort, almost like Augustine's prelinguistic infant, he coos and flails and pours out his heart in the speech of everyday folk. It's probably important that Eckhart was condemned mainly for his German-language teachings. Like a craftsman who has none of his familiar tools, he had to do without Scholastic Latin, but this also freed him to preach in a way that cut and burned. Although his German lacked the subtlety of Latin, it had something that the language of the lecture hall and reference book lacked: the ability to render the spiritual world palpable, sensuous, and tactile through the homely images of the language of the hearth.

Eckhart, like all medieval theologians, read Scripture allegorically, so sermons devoted to the birth of Christ and the finding of Jesus in the temple gave him the opportunity to address what most concerned him: the interior life. How can the Word of God be born within *us*, even now? For Eckhart, the birth of the Word within begins when we recognize that God, as it were, surrounds us, as if (there's that word again, "quasi") exerting pressure on us from all sides—as if we are at the bottom of the ocean—even though (as for Plotinus and Augustine) we're ignorant of this holy weight. But when through ascetical exercise and then through a second stage of intellectual temperance we create space in our hearts, God rushes in to fill the vacuum:

This is . . . what the masters write when they maintain that at the very same moment that the matter of the child in the womb is fully prepared, God pours the living spirit into the body, which is the soul or the body's form. Both happen in a single moment: the being prepared and the inpouring of the soul. When nature has reached its highest point, God bestows his grace, and at the very same moment that the spirit is ready, God enters it, without hesitation or delay. In the Book of Mysteries [Revelation] it is written that our Lord said to the people: "Behold I stand at the door, knocking and waiting. If anyone lets me in, I shall eat with him" (Rev. 3:20). You need to seek him neither here nor there, for he is no further than the door of your heart. There he stands, waiting for someone who is ready to open the door and to let him in. You do not need to call him from far away; he can hardly wait for you to let him in. He desires you a thousand times more urgently than you do him. The opening of the door and his entering in happen in exactly the same moment. (Sermon 4, 226–27)[23]

You can feel the heat radiating from Eckhart's preaching. In this way, throughout his German sermons the university master scours the earth, looking for whatever majestic or homely metaphor will suit his purposes, whether it's the embryo being knit together in the womb of its mother or the lightning bolt striking the earth. Just after the passage quoted above, Eckhart develops a different metaphor to describe God's holy presence:

> You should know that God *must* pour himself into you and act upon you where he finds you prepared. You should not think that God is like a carpenter on earth who works or does not work as he will and for whom it is a matter of choice as to whether he should do something or not, according to his inclination. This is not the case with God who must act and must pour himself into you wherever and whenever he finds you prepared, just as the sun must pour itself forth and cannot hold itself back when the air is pure and clean. Certainly, it would be a major failing if God did not perform great works in you, pouring great goodness into you, in so far as he finds you empty and bare. (Sermon 4, 226)

Eckhart wants to get at that exceptional act in which I push all the "noise" out of my life, and even bring calm to my intellect, to achieve a state of tranquility in which God reveals himself within my heart. My heart becomes a new Bethlehem.

In order to hear this "whispering voice," to hear the "knock" within, I have to push out all the chaos and triviality that ordinarily besets me; I have to become "empty and bare" within. This process of purification begins, on the simplest level, with pious disciplines: vows and fasting and corporal mortification, or sleeping on hard surfaces, or wearing hair shirts—all the good old medieval disciplines (Sermon 4). But we impose discipline on the body, not to punish ourselves but so that our passions will stop distracting us. Throughout his vernacular writings, Eckhart is insistent that we remember that there's a much higher level of spiritual life than pious practice—that is, to be filled with God, to be filled with love. And this is where Eckhart gets really daring, almost trying to dismantle the self-confident pietism of his very devout age.

Eckhart says that if a man is caught in the net of love, his "least action or practice . . . is more pleasing to God than all the works of others who, though free from mortal sin, are inferior to him in love." Whatever the man of love does no longer matters, in one sense: "whether he does anything or nothing it is of no account," because he's tapped into the core of reality (Sermon 4, 60). The whole point of pious activities is to gain inwardness, to walk into the barren desert of the soul, where it's quiet enough to hear God. If you're there, you don't need the pious deeds that got you there: "As long as this inwardness lasts, be it a week, a month, or a year, none of this time is lost by the monk or nun, for God, who has captured and imprisoned them, must answer for it. . . . The least act of God outweighs all the works of creatures" (Sermon 3, 53).

And so, to be filled with God, I need to be in a state of what Eckhart calls "darkness" (that is, pure "potential receptivity," Sermon 4, 56), "silence," or "barrenness." I have to keep myself "empty and bare, just following and tracking this darkness and unknowing without turning back" (Sermon 4, 57). But to remain there, it's not enough to impose a little discipline on my body and on my time. I also have to engage in an act of intellectual abnegation, a disciplined taming of the ambition of the intellect to know and control everything. Eckhart describes, in an almost Augustinian key, the restless hunger of the mind to know and understand. A man will spend a whole year trying to understand a problem (remember, Eckhart's a college professor!), to get to the bottom of it, to discover what "grounds" it. But after we know that ground, we feverishly want to understand something else, and then something else, and so we go looking for the foundation of the next problem—the "grounding" for this and the "ground" for that.

It's similar with the theologian and God. We say a lot of true things about him: God is a spirit. He is omnipotent. He is omniscient. When we begin to parse these ideas, though, they start to seem less like positive attributes and more like encoded assertions of what he is not. "God is spiritual" means he is incorporeal or has no body or mass. "God is omnipotent" could mean that he's not limited in the mode of a created being. But who is God, anyway? Have we come to the end of the road? Have we come to something that the restless intellect cannot find a "ground" for? Our own desire to know and argue and understand can clutter the mind, and prevent the mystical birth of Christ within from taking place. Eckhart likens the clamorous operations of our intellect to an untamed animal. It wants to know! And so it takes a little bit of counteracting force to keep even the truth-seeking intellect within its proper bounds. "A man cannot attain to this birth except by withdrawing his senses from all things. And that requires a mighty effort to drive back the powers of the soul and inhibit their functioning. This must be done with force; without force it cannot be done. As Christ said, 'The kingdom of heaven suffers violence, and the violent take it by force' [Matt. 11:12]" (Sermon 3, 51).

How do you do this? This is where Eckhart becomes sublime: you have to make a "desert" of yourself, to enter into that region of the soul that is pure barrenness. You have to push out all the noise, even the "good" noise of piety and reasoning. You have to "strip" the mind (Sermon 3, 51): "For you have abandoned self and have gone out of your [soul's] powers and their activities, and your personal nature. Therefore, God must enter into your being and powers, because you have bereft yourself of all possessions, and become as a desert, as it is written, 'The voice of one crying in the wilderness' [Matt. 3:3]" (Sermon 3, 52). And when we get there, "ardent, and yet in a detached, quiet stillness," there will be "no need to tell God what [we] need or desire: He already knows" (Sermon 3, 53).

Even among correct opinions about God, it's sometimes hard to find God himself. Think about how hard it was for Mary and Joseph to find a place for the birth of the Son. Thus Eckhart asks whether a man can find

> this birth through particular things which, while divine, are mediated to us from outside by the senses. Certain concepts concerning

> God are an example of this, including the idea that God is good,
> that he is wise, merciful or whatever it may be that reason can de-
> rive from itself and which is similarly divine. Can all this bring us
> the birth? Indeed not. For although it may all be good and of God,
> it is all mediated by the senses from outside. But if this birth is to
> shine out in truth and purity, there must be a movement solely from
> within, from God. All your activity must be stilled. (Sermon 4, 223)

This "barren land" is as empty as the desert of Judea or the wild
places of Wyoming—that is, it's not empty at all! It's just free of
clutter and noise and useless activity. It has a fullness unto itself
that, most of the time, we're too busy to heed. But when we do,
God will irrupt within and the Word will be born within: "Where
does one find peace and rest? There, truly, where there is rejection,
desolation, and estrangement from all creatures" (Sermon 4, 57).

When the miracle of the birth of the Word within occurs, the
soul undergoes a fundamental reorientation toward life. It becomes a soul "from whom God hides nothing," and the vision is
a little startling, because (remember, we are still using metaphors
here) the heart of reality turns out to be like laughter or play. The
groundless ground has no "why"; that is, it doesn't exist for any
reason prior to it, and so it is best captured by activities such as
play and laughter and love (or sunbathing!), activities that we
do without feeling the need to justify them. We do not approach
children who are deeply engaged in some imaginative game and
ask, "Why are you doing this?" (at least not since the Victorian
period). We don't sneak up behind lovers laughing together on
a park bench and ask, "Why are you engaged in this activity?"
At the heart of the universe is pointless superfluity, pure gratuitous abundance, delight, and hilarity. For so many of us, trained
to think of religion as stern and disciplined, this is shattering.
There's something more important than being good? Yes. When
I see God in his pure delight, the one who is "without a why,"
and I clear space for that vision within my soul, I too can live, in
Eckhart's extraordinary phrase, "without a why." The relation-

ship between my activities is inverted: now it's not that I'm good in order to get to God; rather, because I'm in God I overflow into good works. Or, in Eckhart's startling formulation, I see God in all things. Every action I undertake is no longer *because of* something else. Rather, it's something that flows forth from me, almost as an excess (Sermon 3).

Throughout his sermons Eckhart tends to take Augustinian truisms—such as "God is nearer to me than I am to myself"—and radicalize them. How is God "nearer to me" than I am to myself? Eckhart's answer is that my inner world is the inner world of the Trinity (Sermon 13). In this way, Eckhart suggests, "the eye with which I see God is the same eye with which God sees me: my eye and God's eye are one eye, one seeing, one knowing and one love" (Sermon 57, 298). Eckhart is so close to Paul and Augustine. Indeed, he praises Paul for giving up everything in the world for God: "He left everything that he could get from God, he left everything that God could give him and everything he might receive from God. In leaving these he left God for God, and then God was left with him" (Sermon 57, 296). In other words, when we "strip" ourselves of everything but our divine filiation, when the one thing we treasure is Jesus Christ within us, then we come to be the heirs of that which Christ himself is owed! In this sense, the whole treasury of holiness is now open to us. Eckhart describes that inner treasury in this way:

> "God has sent his Only-Begotten Son into the world." You must not by this understand the external world in which the Son ate and drank with us, but understand it to apply to the inner world. As truly as the Father in his simple nature gives his Son birth naturally, so truly does he give him birth in the most inward part of the spirit, and that is the inner world. Here God's ground is my ground, and my ground is God's ground. Here I live from what is my own, as God lives from what is his own. Whoever has looked for an instant into this ground, to such a man a thousand marks of red, minted gold are no more than a counterfeit penny. It is

out of this inner ground that you should perform all your works without asking, "Why?" I say truly: So long as you perform your works for the sake of the kingdom of heaven, or for God's sake, or for the sake of your eternal blessedness, and you work them from without, you are going completely astray. You may well be tolerated, but it is not the best. Because truly, when people think that they are acquiring more of God in inwardness, in devotion, in sweetness and in various approaches than they do by the fireside or in the stable, you are acting just as if you took God and muffled his head up in a cloak and pushed him under a bench. . . . If anyone went on for a thousand years asking of life: "Why are you living?" life, if it could answer, would only say: "I live so that I may live." That is because life lives out of its own ground and springs from its own source, and so it lives without asking why it is itself living. If anyone asked a truthful man who works out of his own ground: "Why are you performing your works?" and if he were to give a straight answer, he would only say, "I work so that I may work." (Sermon 13)[24]

These are dizzying words. When we are willing to dwell in the desert, there we can "hear the eternal Word"; more importantly, God rushes out, seeks us out, dwells in us as if we were in him. Echoing Dionysius, Eckhart says, "God is in such haste to get us and hurries so much as if His divine being would be shattered and destroyed in itself, that He may reveal to us the abysm of His Godhead and plenitude of His being and His nature: God then hastens to make it our own just as it is His own. Here God has delight and joy in abundance" (Sermon 57, 295–96). And a single moment of such an encounter is worth three worlds over, a biblical idea (see 1 Cor. 2:9) that Eckhart gets at with another homespun analogy: imagine a poor man with nothing to give but who feels in his heart that if he had three worlds in his possession he would have no trouble giving them all up for God. Such a man will be treated by God as if he had really given them all away (Sermon 57).

Reading Eckhart is exhilarating. He's so immediate, sensuous, palpable, tactile, and thus shocking. His preaching is accessible and quotable. Although there are, it is true, important metaphysical differences between Eckhart and, say, Augustine (Eckhart is almost like Plotinus on the relationship between the soul and God), this rock hammer—who preaches "living without a why," who preaches "living in the desert," who preaches the giddy delight of a God who wishes to share the fullness of his joy with us—can disturb our spiritual somnolence.[25] In other words, Eckhart makes the wild promises of the Bible seem strange again. Or, to put it in Eckhart's own intoxicating prose: "But God's comfort is pure and unmixed: it is perfect and complete, and He is so eager to give it to you that He cannot wait to give you Himself first of all. God is so besotted in His love for us, it is just as if He had forgotten heaven and earth and all His blessedness and all His Godhead and had no business except with me alone, to give me everything for my comforting. And He gives it to me complete, He gives it to me perfectly, He gives it to me more purely, He gives it to me all the time, and He gives it to all creatures" (Sermon 91, 446).

But it's hard to get this, in part because we have to be willing to give up even the experience of "religiousness." Eckhart imagines a Christian looking around, noticing that others seem to be progressing in the Christian life while he himself has stalled. Eckhart advises that we thank God for their sake and continue on gratefully without his special assistance! "Intend only him and have no thought as to whether it is you or God who performs things in you."[26] Choosing God, even at the expense of feeling religious. Choosing God, even in a landscape of desolation.

5

Praying with the Whole World

Natural Contemplation and the Legacy of the Desert Fathers

The man who truly prays is the man who sees the place of God. This is what it means to be a theologian.

—Evagrius, *Kephalaia Gnostika*

Truly the visible is the manifest image [*eikōn*] of the invisible.
—Dionysius the Areopagite, "Letter 10"

The Desert Fathers and Mothers

In the fourth century there was a strange but inspiring flight of heroic souls from ancient cities out into the solitude of the surrounding deserts of Egypt and Anatolia: Macarius the Great, Anthony of Egypt, Macarius of Alexandria, and a whole host of other curiously named Greek and Syrian "abbas" (or desert "fathers")—Abba Pambo, Abba Serapion, Abba Nilus, Poemen the Shepherd, and many others. They were a loosely organized

band of Christian fugitives from the world who had become convinced that life in the sophisticated and cosmopolitan cities of the
ancient world (e.g., Alexandria, Constantinople, Babylon, and
Rome) was corrupting, so they went out to the desert to seek
intensity, simplicity, and authenticity. Gregory the Great, in his
Life of Benedict, picked up the theme two centuries later: "While
still living in the world . . . he saw how barren it was with its at-
tractions. . . . [He] abandoned his studies to go into solitude."[1]
Another monk would call it "voluntary exile."[2]

As the fame of the desert fathers and mothers grew, curious and
eager city dwellers began to seek them out to ask for wise advice.
Just as a CEO or Hollywood celebrity might go to India or Tibet
to ask for a word of wisdom from some aged and mellow Buddhist
monk who has gained a reputation for wisdom and enlightenment,
so too did curious, and sometimes important, citizens go out to the
surrounding desert to ask for a word from the sages who lived there.
In this way the sayings of the desert fathers have been preserved
for us—a hodgepodge of fascinating and unpredictable stories,
mottoes, one-liners, enigmatic sayings, and wise words for how
to achieve sanctity.[3] For instance, one monk by the name of Abba
Pambo gained a reputation for holiness. *The Sayings of the Desert
Fathers* tells us that "there was a monk named Pambo and they said
of him that he spent three years saying to God, 'Do not glorify me
on earth.' God glorified him so that one could not gaze steadfastly
at him because of the glory of his countenance" (*Sayings*, 196:1).[4]
Not surprisingly, people began to visit him to see what he knew:

> Two brethren came to see Abba Pambo one day and the first asked
> him, "Abba, I fast for two days then I eat two loaves; am I saving
> my soul or am I going the wrong way?" The second said, "Abba,
> every day I get two pence from my manual work, and I keep a
> little for my food and give the rest in alms; shall I be saved or
> shall I be lost?" They remained a long time questioning him and
> still the old man gave them no reply. After four days they had to
> leave and the priest comforted them saying, "Do not be troubled,

brothers, God gives the reward. It is the old man's custom not to speak readily till God inspires him." So they went to see the old man and said to him, "Abba, pray for us." He said to them . . . , "If Pambo fasted for two days together and ate two loaves, would he become a monk that way? No. . . . The works are good, but if you guard your conscience towards your neighbor, then you will be saved." They were satisfied and went away joyfully. (*Sayings*, 196:2)

Intrigued by the reputations of such holy sages, Christians from the cities would go out to their simple huts in the desert to ask them all sorts of questions about the good life, prayer, and sacrifice. And some of these desert dwellers were so impressive that the city dwellers would stay and become their disciples. The life they would take up would be founded on absolute simplicity, solitude, sincerity, and what we today would call mindfulness, because it was the goal of the desert dwellers to remain in constant conversation with God: "Someone asked Abba Anthony, 'What must one do in order to please God?' The old man replied, 'Pay attention to what I tell you: whoever you may be, always have God before your eyes'" (*Sayings*, 2:2). But to get there, you have to get the mind to stop racing, stop looking down on other people, stop worrying about current events and future security, stop fretting over old family wounds—and you have to stop networking, using, craving, lusting. That's hard.

Armed with this desire for purity and inner peace (what they called *apatheia*, borrowing a term from the ancient Greeks), the desert sages warred against the addictive, anxious, craving tendencies within and set out to lead a hard life of grinding down their passions through solitude, simplicity, and fasting. And they clung to these principles with all their might. For example, one of the *Sayings* tells us:

It was said of Abba Theodore of Pherme that the three things he held to be fundamental were: poverty, asceticism, and flight from men. (*Sayings*, 74:5)

And:

> Abba Poemen said, "In Abba Pambo we see three bodily activities: abstinence from food until the evening every day, silence, and much manual work." (*Sayings*, 188:150)

And:

> Abba Pambo asked Abba Anthony: "What ought I to do?" and the old man said to him, "Do not trust in your own righteousness, do not worry about the past, but control your tongue and your stomach." (*Sayings*, 2:6)

Elsewhere, the same Abba Anthony adds,

> Just as fish die if they stay too long out of water, so the monks who loiter outside their cells or pass their time with men of the world lose the intensity of inner peace. . . . We must hurry to reach our cell, for fear that if we delay outside we will lose our interior watchfulness. (*Sayings*, 2:3)

Were the sages socially awkward and extreme? Absolutely. Did they have allergic reactions to every kind of faking? Yes. But they achieved something that we in a consumerist culture sometimes find ourselves longing for: stillness—real stillness—and deep peace.[5] But they also recognized how easy it is to lose that inner stillness. And so they settled down to a long life of hard work, discipline, and even abstinence from speaking. "They said of Abba Or that he never lied, nor swore, nor hurt anyone, nor spoke without necessity" (*Sayings*, 246:2). Abba Or added this himself: "He who is honored and praised beyond his merits will suffer much condemnation, but he who is held as of no account among men will receive glory in heaven" (*Sayings*, 247:10). These desert sages thought of themselves as athletes or soldiers in training (see Abba Serapion, *Sayings*, 227:3). And over the course of time they became distrustful of themselves, so that they even tried to escape their own reputations!

[A] magistrate came to visit [Abba Simon]. The clergy went on ahead and said to the old man, "Abba, get ready, for this magistrate has heard of you and is coming for your blessing." So he said, "Yes, I will prepare myself." Then he put on a rough habit and taking some bread and cheese in his hands he went and sat in the doorway to eat it. When the magistrate arrived with his suite and saw him, he despised him and said, "Is this the anchorite of whom we have heard so much?" And they went away at once. (*Sayings*, 225:2)

Evagrius and Deep Knowledge of the Created Universe

And thus we come to yet another flavor of mysticism. If Augustine gave us a mysticism of love in which we come to see God by means of affection, and Dionysius and Gregory and Eckhart gave us an intellectualist vision by which we purify the mind, sometimes even of correct opinion, the desert fathers and those they inspired (especially in Benedictine monasticism) give us a picture of the "athlete of God," one who wrestles against demons and the passions. As Evagrius of Pontus puts it, "Wrestlers are not the only ones whose occupation it is to throw others down and to be thrown in turn; the demons, too, wrestle—with us."[6]

Evagrius (345–399/400) had enjoyed a meteoric rise in the greatest city in the world, Constantinople, but because of a humiliating affair with a married woman, his career came crashing down. And so he left the city, the city that was full of false dreams and pretentious posturing. After a short time in Nitria, Egypt, he moved even farther out to Kellia, where he lived the rest of his life seeking "a habit of contemplation that is not easily lost."[7]

Importantly, Evagrius brought with him into this Wild West of the Egyptian desert his sophisticated background and learning. He had been a student of Platonism and Stoicism, and he was particularly indebted to Origen and Clement of Alexandria. Thus, throughout his extensive writings, we can see him bringing a sense of order to the jumble of wise sayings and enigmatic stories of his predecessors in the desert: "It is . . . necessary to make diligent enquiry of the upright ways of the monks who have gone before us and to correct ourselves with respect to these, for one can find many noble things said and done by them" (*Praktikos* 91, 112). In particular, Evagrius contributes two things to our understanding of mysticism: (1) a subtle explanation for how the demons get at our inner psychic lives and, thus, how we can resist them; and (2) the ancient teaching on the progressive stages of ascent from this world to the next. For this reason Evagrius is sometimes said to have realized "the first complete system of Christian spirituality."[8]

According to Evagrius, the mind is rarely at peace because it is constantly assailed by imagining what could have been, what could be, and what should be. These internal and disquieting "vain imaginings" (*logismoi*) are brought about when we enter into the "magnetic field" of demons, who cast a kind of field of influence. When I come into this field, I find that the tenor of my hopes and dreams and desires has been affected on the level of the imagination. Under this influence, it now becomes weirdly easy to fixate on frustrations, be anxious about the future, caress some ancient wound, or be offended by someone whom I have given myself over to hating. It is hard to keep my mind at peace; I'm fidgety and irritable, and thus I cannot pray. In prayer the soul should become transparent to the love of God, or, as Evagrius memorably puts it, our souls become like a sapphire.[9] And thus the most important question we can ask ourselves at the first level of spiritual training is this: What can I do to make sure I don't lose the sense of tranquility and stillness that is the necessary condition for such prayerfulness?[10] Under the influence of "vain imaginings" (*logismoi*), my mind loses its sapphire-like transparency and undergoes what Evagrius calls a "thickening" process. The demons try to head off my entry into prayer by making sure I fall into "imaginings" first: "Why do the demons want to produce in us gluttony, fornication, avarice, anger, and resentment, and the other passions? So that the mind becomes thickened by them and unable to pray as it ought."[11] We have to be able to recognize these false dreams and bitter memories and excessive or misdirected longings when we experience them. Enter Evagrius the psychologist, who, even though writing in the 300s AD, could be a modern-day therapist.

In the best version of myself, I long for God. In my best self, I choose the harder path, a path of discipline. But when I come under demonic influence—when I am breathing the air of their spell—I begin to quietly doubt the wisdom of my "rash" choice to follow God. If I had once wanted to fast so that I could experience creation with gratitude, now I have doubts and wonder whether I have been too zealous: "The thought of gluttony . . . describes for [the monk] his stomach, his liver and spleen, dropsy and lengthy illness, the scarcity of necessities and the absence of doctors" (*Praktikos* 7, 98). Under the guise of sober and rational concerns, I am subtly seduced to overinflate the delicacy of my health and regard it as excessively precious; my resolve starts to slide a little bit, and my transparency to God thickens.

But there are other *logismoi* (internal images that stir up the passions): "Avarice suggests a lengthy old age, inability to perform manual labour, famines that will come along, diseases that will arise, the bitter realities of poverty" (*Praktikos* 9, 98). When I sit down to pray, I sometimes realize that there are many real-world issues that need my attention: global pandemics, elections, stock markets, international affairs. I soon realize that a nervous anxiety, like a worm, has insinuated itself into my heart. And then there's good old-fashioned anger, "a movement directed against one who has done injury" or, Evagrius devastatingly adds, "is thought to have done so" (*Praktikos* 11, 99). In my "vain imaginings" (*logismoi*), I sometimes don't care whether what I'm upset about is real or made up. I'm secretly addicted to the feeling of being wounded, and sometimes this feeling erupts in rage: "a furnace for the heart, an eruption of flames . . . a mother of wild beasts" (*On the Vices* 5). Elsewhere, though, Evagrius adds a word about how to be "politely" hateful: "When the demons see that we have not been inflamed to the boiling point of offences, then rising up in a moment of stillness they pry open the ruling faculty so that we may treat impudently in their absence those whom we treated irenically in their presence" (*To Eulogios* 5, 32).

In addition to our tendency to coddle our fears about our health, to fret about the future, and to give in to anger, we can suffer the vain imaginings of jealousy ("the root of slander, the coveting of cheerfulness, the feigning of friendship, treachery in confidence, hatred of love," *On the Vices* 8). We can dream unrealistically of future importance ("Vainglory involves fantasizing about social encounters, a pretence of industriousness . . . desire for privilege, the ultimate title, slavery to praises," *On the Vices* 7). Or we are overcome by sadness: "Sadness is one who dwells over loss, who is familiar with frustrated acquisition . . . a reminder of insult, and a darkening of the soul" (*On the Vices* 4). And far too many of us know about lust, the inclination to so radically reduce someone to a piece of flesh that it is possible to lie in a "bed of dreams" longing for "unfeeling sexual congress" (*On the Vices* 2).

Of all the temptations he discusses, though, Evagrius is at his best when describing so-called acedia, that strange spiritual lethargy in which I flirt with every excuse there is to justify not doing what is already within my power. I begin to give in to the feeling that the people I'm around don't inspire or appreciate me. I have a feeling that there are other places where I could flourish if I got a chance for a fresh start. If my boss weren't so . . . ; if the people at my church weren't so . . . ; if my pastor didn't . . . —then I could use my talents. And so I'm left with the feeling that any given day is an infinitely long patch of silence that I have to endure while no one notices or cares what *I'm* going through:

> The demon of acedia, also called the noonday demon (cf. Ps. 90:6), is the most oppressive of all the demons. He attacks the monk about the fourth hour [10 a.m.] and besieges his soul until the eighth hour [2 p.m.]. First of all, he makes it appear that the sun moves slowly or not at all, and that the day seems to be fifty hours long. Then he compels the monk to look constantly towards the windows, to jump out of the cell, to watch the sun to see how far

it is from the ninth hour [3 p.m.], to look this way and that. . . .
And further, he instills in him a dislike for the place and for his
state of life itself, for manual labour, and also the idea that love
has disappeared from among the brothers and there is no one to
console him. . . . [The demon] leads him on to a desire for other
places where he can easily find the wherewithal to meet his needs.
(*Praktikos* 12, 99)

I challenge anyone to tell me that this insight, written about sev-
enteen hundred years ago, is now out of date.

Evagrius's descriptions of these "vain imaginings" (*logismoi* as
opposed to *logoi*) are convincing, I think, but he adds another brilliant insight: these demonically inspired disturbances and desires
are a coordinated squad of temptations, so that just as we get over
some "hot" sin (like lust or gluttony) we are assailed by a "cold"
one (sadness or jealousy or vainglory). Evagrius was the first to
formulate the "seven deadly sins" (or "capital vices"), although he
thought of them as eight: gluttony, lust, avarice, sadness (acedia),
anger, vainglory, jealousy, and pride.

If this is the diagnosis, what is the treatment? Spiritual quar-
antine. We have to struggle and fight and pray as well as fast
(Evagrius says he ate only once per day). We have to stay away
from places of vanity, we have to meditate, and we have to spend
time in friendship. Most importantly, we have to fill up the soul
with those virtues that are the opposite of soul-sickening images of
desire. Instead of fornication, we need chastity: "a robe of truth,
. . . a charioteer for the eyes, an overseer for one's thinking, . . . a
lantern for the heart and an inclination for prayer" (*On the Vices*
2). Instead of avarice, we need "freedom from possessions . . . , a
life free of suffering, a treasure free of envy, a heaven free of care"
(*On the Vices* 3). Joy, in the meantime, destroys sorrow: "happiness from doing good, an ornament of renunciation, a receptacle
of hospitality" (*On the Vices* 4).

As we have said, though, the goal of this stripped-down simplicity and discipline is the cultivation of a spirit of stillness, a quiet,

tranquil silence of the heart—what Evagrius, borrowing a term from ancient Stoic philosophers, calls *apatheia*. Evagrius's pupil John Cassian (360–435), writing in Latin, calls it "purity of heart" (*puritas cordis*) and defines it in this beautiful way:

> Having crucified all wrongful desires, with no concern for the present, no thought about personal likings, no anxiety about the future, he remains undisturbed by avarice, pride, contentiousness, envy, or remembrance of wrongs. While still in the body, he is dead to all material and earthly elements. . . . No 'image' . . . of former or prospective sins haunts the memory or imagination.[12]

To finally have a heart at rest! To no longer be at odds with yourself! To be in a state of *apatheia* or *puritas cordis* is to no longer feel envious about your best friend's success or be peevish and negative and depressed even when you are surrounded by gifts. It's also to be free from spiritual fidgeting. But the hard path to *puritas cordis* is *askesis* or *praktike*—that is, the active life of wrestling and struggling and fighting and crying out in the desert, where my head is clear.

That is the first useful piece of theoretical systematizing that the former city boy, Evagrius, did for his practical-minded brothers out in the deserts of Egypt. But he also reminded them that the acquisition of *apatheia* is not an end in itself. There's no point in having virtue just to have virtue. Discipline and *askesis* are pursued to achieve *apatheia* (purity of heart, peace from the passions); but the point of possessing purity of heart is to gain something that now strikes us as quite incredible: the ability to enter into a state of "natural contemplation," what Evagrius calls "deep knowledge of the created universe." Here's how he outlines the progressively ascending steps of the spiritual life:

> The fear of God strengthens faith, my son, and continence in turn strengthens this fear. Patience and hope make this latter virtue solid beyond all shaking and they also give birth to *apatheia*. Now

this *apatheia* has a child called *love* who keeps the door to deep knowledge of the created universe. (*Praktikos* 8, 96)

"Deep knowledge of the created universe": this is what Evagrius and Cassian call *theoria physike* or "natural contemplation."[13] In other words, if my human powers and desires can be attuned to one another so that I find lasting spiritual calm, then I can enter into harmony with the rest of creation. The desert monks believed that in our sinful state we are exiled not only from our true selves but also from participating harmoniously with the rest of creation. But people of *apatheia* (stillness) can begin to listen to the essences of creatures (to "hear" their *logoi*, their true essences, as opposed to perverted "vain imaginings" of them). They can begin to hear, as it were, the inner song of creation and make its song their own, turning the voiceless drone of creation into a hymn of praise to God.

Thus, for Evagrius, once you have detached your passions from creaturely goods, you can, for the first time, step back and see these creatures differently, as beautiful in their own way, possessing their own purposes—ends and meanings distinct from their mere utility to you. The American monk Thomas Merton (1915–1968), who wrote a famous modern *Confessions*, *The Seven Storey Mountain*, accurately captures this ancient Christian belief. Merton became interested in the idea of natural contemplation, and in an unpublished course he gave in the early 1960s to novices at the Abbey of Gethsemani in Kentucky, he dedicated a lecture to natural contemplation. He said that natural contemplation is the recovery of the Edenic mode of consciousness: "Things have an inner logic placed there by their Creator. The artist must be sensitive to the unique voice or vocation of each being and must vigorously protest when things are being prevented from attaining their spiritual end by misuse." For Merton, we will be held accountable for the "systematic obscuring and desecration of the *logoi* of things and of their sacred meaning."[14]

The ancient monastic ideal of natural contemplation inspired Merton, so he asked his superior for permission to seek deeper solitude. The abbot made him the forester, and Merton moved into a hermitage deep in the woods to live in contemplative solitude. He described his life in silence as his quest to "recover paradise." In a book about the Cistercian order, he wrote, "When the monks had found their homes, they not only settled there, for better or for worse, but they sank their roots into the ground and fell in love with their woods. . . . Forest and field, sun and wind and sky, earth and water, all speak the same silent language, reminding the monk that he is here to develop like the things that grow all around him."[15] In fact, such an ideal became so important to Merton that he began to describe his life of solitude as a marriage between him and the woods:

> Like everyone else I live under the bomb. But unlike most people I live in the woods. Do not ask me to explain this. I am embarrassed to describe it. . . .
> I live in the woods out of necessity. I get out of bed in the middle of the night because it is imperative that I hear the silence of the night, alone, and, with my face on the floor, say psalms, alone, in the silence of the night.
> It is necessary for me to live here alone without a woman, for the silence of the forest is my bride and the sweet dark warmth of the whole world is my love and out of the heart of that dark warmth comes the secret that is heard only in silence, but it is the root of all the secrets that are whispered by all the lovers in their beds all over the world.[16]

Such sentiments, although they often strike us as strange, are in fact millennia old, originally coming from the desert fathers of Egypt and then through medieval Italian monasticism. These ideas would eventually take root in the Russian Orthodox tradition, influencing Fyodor Dostoyevsky, who was particularly moved by another of Evagrius's followers, Isaac of Syria, a monk who described being reunited to the whole of creation:

> An elder was once asked, "What is a compassionate heart?" He replied: "It is a heart on fire for the whole of creation, for humanity,

for the birds, for the animals, for demons and for all that exists. At the recollection and at the sight of them such a person's eyes overflow with tears owing to the vehemence of compassion that grips his heart. . . . That is why he constantly offers up prayers full of tears, even for the irrational animals and for the enemies of truth, even for those who harm him. . . . He even prays for the reptiles as a result of the great compassion which is poured out beyond measure—after the likeness of God—in his heart."[17]

In this sense, what the apostle Paul calls "the groaning of creation" (Rom. 8:22–24) becomes a hymn in me: what nature longs to say but cannot, I can give voice to, and thus my own smallness of being can be dramatically enlarged. The world's "prayer" can become mine, and thus my own meager efforts are magnified.

But even as I delight in the *logoi* or inner essences of things in the world through natural contemplation, my mind moves from a kind of admiration of *things* to gratitude directed toward the Source of being. As my mind soars over the ocean of creation, admiring all those things contained within, it may sometimes rise even higher and take delight in the essence of all those things. At this point my mind begins to "flicker" up and down between natural contemplation and *theologia*—that is, not academic theology (saying correct things about God) but a kind of "God-speak" in which I inhale his fragrance and exhale gratitude. This is the final stage of the ascent: *theologia*, a kind of deep prayer. Thus, natural contemplation bleeds into prayer. Evagrius imagines that it is like when many rivers of different colors and tastes flow into the great sea. All those *logoi* in the world I had been admiring and delighting in flow together into a single source, a great ocean of delight:

> Anyone who stands on the seashore is seized by amazement at its limitlessness, taste, colour and all it contains, and at how the rivers, torrents and streams that pour into it become limitless and undifferentiated in it, since they acquire all its properties. It is likewise for anyone who considers the end of the intellects: he will be greatly amazed and marvel as he beholds all these various

different knowledges uniting themselves in the one uniquely real knowledge and beholds them all become this one without end.[18]

Elsewhere, Evagrius changes the metaphor and describes this experience of prayer as a great sky during the summertime that opens itself up within my heart: "In pure thought there lie impressed a sky/heaven, luminous to see, and a vast region."[19] The visible world doesn't disappear, and I don't come to despise it; but an interior world seems to open up within.

And so we have a three-stage process of ascent that, with variations, is repeated again and again in the later tradition:

1. A stage concerned with practices and habits, repeating the right moral actions, and undergoing asceticism (*askesis* or *praktike*). This is the stage in which, like a musician obsessively practicing major scales with their harmonic minors, I practice the basic scales of detachment.

2. A higher stage of *theoria physike*—that is, "natural contemplation," when I have begun to listen in on the meaning of creation.

3. *Theologia*, what I am translating very literally as "God-speak," the moment that, after the beauties of the world have pooled up in my mind, I find myself drifting toward the Creator in ineffable gratitude.

This is the upward life of the desert: to achieve calm so that I can become entranced with the rhythmic beauty of the world and forget about my anxieties and preoccupations, just as when I am overcome by the sound of the sea and denuded of my usual anxieties. And then I am just steps away from true prayer, *theologia*, where I can dwell in the presence of God. This prayer can erupt suddenly within us—or, rather, we are snatched up into it. We are pulled up into a "space" that has no color or image, Evagrius says mysteriously: "The mind, . . . when it is engaged in knowledge, it spends its time in contemplation, and when it is in prayer, it is in a light without form, which is called the place of God." We are lifted up and stand before God in the nudity of our souls. For this reason, Evagrius says, "If you are a theologian, you will pray truly; and if you pray truly, you will be a theologian."[20]

But the important thing to emphasize with Evagrius is that we can't skip ahead to *theologia*, to that opening sky and horizonless sea. If you want deep prayer, you must have a "naked intellect," which means you must rejoin the world in its natural prayer (natural contemplation). You must cleanse your heart of sadness and petty anger and vain self-importance and lust and addictions of all kinds: "The mind [cannot] see the place of God within itself, unless it has transcended all the mental representations associated with objects. Nor will it transcend them, if it has not put off the passions that bind it to sensible objects through mental representations."[21]

This rich and strange idea of the enlargement of my being through the prayerful love of the creatures of this world particularly flourished in the Byzantine East, but it wasn't absent from the Latin West. In the next sections of this chapter I will treat two proponents of natural contemplation in the medieval West: Hugh of St. Victor and Francis of Assisi (as interpreted by Bonaventure).

How to Read the World: from Benedict to Hugh of St. Victor

The most foundational document of the early medieval period in the Latin West was Saint Benedict's *Rule*. This new, modified version of the spiritual vision of the desert—a communal, stern-minded, disciplined pursuit of "perfect obedience"—swept across Europe and dictated the dominant form of religious practice until the age of the mendicants and Scholasticism (the thirteenth century). In some ways, the differences between the loosely associated hermits in the Greek-speaking desert and their Latin-speaking successors in continental Europe mirror the differences between the quarrelsome but brilliant assembly of individual city-states in classical Greece and the Roman Republic and Empire with its order and laws. Benedict's followers were builders, organizers, lawmakers, and cultivators. They suppressed their personalities for the corporate good. And this mindset is already evident in Benedict's *Rule*.[22]

In his *Rule*, Benedict sets out a blueprint for a *schola servitii*, which I translate loosely as "a boot camp for discipline." The key words in Benedict's *Rule* are "obedience" and "discipline" and "fear." The abbot is reminded to "always remember that at the fearful judgment of God, not only his teaching but also his disciples' obedience will come under scrutiny" (*Rule* 2). The monks are instructed to tear out their own will, like pulling noxious weeds from a garden: "Truly, we are forbidden to do our own will" (*Rule* 7). "[Monks should] no longer live by their own judgment, giving in to their whims and appetites; rather they walk according to another's decisions and directions" (*Rule* 5). Obedience is the right answer in every situation: "obedience under difficult, unfavorable, or even unjust conditions, his heart quietly embrac[ing] suffering" (*Rule* 7). Indeed, some people can be helped only "by blows or some other physical punishment" (*Rule* 2). Meanwhile, the monk must cultivate a sense of fear and distrust of himself: "He must constantly remember everything God has commanded, keeping in mind that all who despise God will burn in hell for their sins, and all who fear God have everlasting life, . . . [guarding] himself at every moment from sins and vices of thought or tongue" (*Rule* 7). The great enemy of a monk's potential success is *voluntas* (his likes and preferences). The Sarabaites are "disgraceful monks" because "their law is what they like to do, whatever strikes their fancy" (*Rule* 1). "In the monastery no one is to follow his own heart's desire" (*Rule* 3).

This is a stern document: "Do not pamper yourself, but love fasting. . . . Speak no foolish chatter, nothing just to provoke laughter; do not love immoderate or boisterous laughter. . . . Every day with tears and sighs confess your past sins. . . . Hate the urgings of self-will" (*Rule* 4). No laughter, no jokes, no "self-actualization," no concerns with your individuality or dreams or ambitions. What is needed is "obedience without delay" (*Rule 5*). Monks "may not have the free disposal even of their own bodies and wills" (*Rule 33*). No relaxation or de-stressing ("Idleness is the enemy of the soul," *Rule 48*); no "idle talk" or "varied reading" (*Rule 48*). Rather, "the life of a monk ought to be a continuous Lent" (*Rule 49*). This is *askesis* in its purest form: distilled discipline. It was the same discipline demanded of a Roman centurion, but now applied to the *miles Christi* (soldier of Christ).

Benedict was a reader of Cassian—he recommends him in the *Rule*—so he had to have known about natural contemplation. Every now and then in the *Rule*, we do in fact see love looking through the cracks of the austere life: "Now, therefore, after ascending all these steps of humility, the monk will quickly arrive at that *perfect love* of God which *casts out fear* (1 John 4:18). Through this love, all that he once performed with dread, he will now begin to observe without effort, as though naturally, from habit, no longer out of fear of hell, but out of love for Christ" (*Rule 7*). But this vision of love—let alone "natural contemplation"—is not within the purview of the *Rule*. That's for later. Maybe. Benedict is content to leave natural contemplation and "the music of the spheres" to "graduate students" in the spiritual life, and only on an as-needed basis. He prefers to keep it simple ("Keep this little rule that we have written for beginners," *Rule 73*), to err on the side of distrust of ourselves. Maybe it's better not to talk too much about natural contemplation. Maybe it's better just to emphasize how long the road of *askesis* really is. In short, when you read the *Rule* it feels like there's a huge gap between that first stage of *askesis* and its partial reward, dwelling at one with the world in its loveliness.

We have to keep this stern Benedictine background in mind to appreciate the spiritual vitality of Hugh of St. Victor and Francis of Assisi, both of whom helped find a new place for natural contemplation, although in very different ways. Hugh was an academic theologian from what is modern-day Germany who joined the newly founded Abbey of St. Victor and became its most remarkable product and spokesman (analogous to what Bernard of Clairvaux was for the Cistercian order). Francis, before his conversion, was a spoiled rich kid who was interested in the popular culture of his day (in Bonaventure's *Life* he's always singing French love songs!) and a bit impetuous but endowed with a native sense of generosity and concern for human suffering. Francis became, though, what the tradition had called an "athlete of God," and developed prodigious amounts of self-control. But both men created space in the West for natural contemplation to come back.

Hugh of St. Victor (1096–1141) lived in an age in which there was a convergence of a series of ancient streams from the classical and late antique worlds. The twelfth century was the "Age of Boethius" (a revival of critical interest in Boethius), a new golden age of Platonism (the *Timaeus* was copied and commented on one hundred times in the 1100s), and a time that included the rediscovery of Dionysius the Areopagite (Hugh was the first of many twelfth- and thirteenth-century Latin writers to produce a commentary on the Byzantine mystic). In other words, all the fragmented materials that Boethius himself had tried to reassemble— like a mosaic shattered into tesserae after an earthquake—were now available again.[23]

The central point that Hugh seems to have taken from Dionysius is the teaching on the iconic nature of the universe, which Hugh neatly sums up in the motto *per visibilia ad invisibilia* (through visible things to invisible things)—which he paired with Augustine's Platonic meditation on Romans 1:20. At the same time, Hugh was also a recipient of the tradition of the liberal arts (as such, he was an intellectual grandson of Alcuin and the Carolingian revival). Hugh, like any good teacher, inflicted chronology, geography, and the rules of grammar and geometry on his religiously minded students, and he expected them to like those subjects as much as he did. We have a precious testimony of what it must have been like to watch him in the classroom, flying around and energetically teaching his students how to memorize bits and pieces of a map. Patrick Gautier Dalché discovered a text that seems to be a classroom lecture by Hugh concerning a map hanging in the room: "Let us examine now the other part of Europe," Hugh says, "which is situated between the Alps and the British sea in the west, and from the south and southeast of Spain towards the north as far as the Riphean mountains and the Maeotis Palus, and let us start with these mountains and the northern marshes."[24] Hugh circles around a space on the map, identifies its boundaries, and points to how each geographical feature is connected to another by using grammatical ligatures such as "and then," "after that," and "from X to Y."[25] In other words, he seems to want his students to get the map into their own heads so that they can close their eyes and see it. And he was equally demanding on them in other subjects: they had to have mental acuity and powerful memories in order to retain history, grammar, and geometry. And he wanted it all assembled into a whole. But to what end?

For Hugh, such muscular memory and highly developed imagination were hardly ends in themselves. When we have gone through the hard work of getting facts into our brains and assembled them all into a coherent whole, then we're ready for contemplation—that is, to hear the voice of God in creation or (more faithful to Hugh's language) find the footprints of God in creation. We have another great example of what this way of learning might have looked like in Hugh's classroom, one that comes from a dialogue and devotional treatise, *On the Vanity of the World* (*De vanitate mundi*), in which he undertakes the Augustinian task of trying to convince a pupil that the invisible world is superior to the sensible. At one point the master puts the imaginative capacity of his disciple to work with more ambitious aims in mind—namely, the internalization of the image of the whole world:

> *Student*: Let's begin then, since I now see the whole universe conjured up before me, and whatever you want to point out to me among all these things I will see without delay and without any difficulty.

> *Teacher*: Do you see then this world?

Student: Very well. Never have I envisioned it so well, since never have I gazed with such ardent affection.

Teacher: What then is shown to you? What is its appearance?

Student: So very beautiful. I am in awe at this work of God.

Teacher: You will find God wondrously within all these things.[26]

Having coached his student in building up an image of the world in the mind, the instructor then conducts a series of thought experiments to promote a "higher" form of looking. Hugh explicitly describes how such interior image-building leads directly to the awakening of what he calls "the eye of the heart":

> *Teacher*: The eye of the body, the higher it is, and the higher the place where it is located, the better and the more broadly it can pour out its rays. It is easier to cast forth rays of the eye when the gaze of vision is sent down from above. . . . But I don't want you to think about the vision of this eye when you hear yourself invited to look. You have within you another kind of eye, an inner one, which is much brighter than this one, which regards past, present, and future things, all at once. . . . Now, since the eye of flesh cannot take these things in all at once . . . it is not the eye of flesh that should be prepared for this vision, but the eye of the heart. Now set yourself in a kind of watchtower of the mind; now send forth the gaze of the mind out and around this world and let your gaze send forth its rays of light everywhere, so that the entirety of the world is placed before the gaze, and then I will reveal to you everything, things which you were ignorant of before, or, at least, if you had seen them, you did not know why they were the way they are.

> *Student*: I must confess that nothing in the universe is hidden from the gaze of the viewer, since the eyes of the heart are opened for such ardent gazing.[27]

But Hugh's most interesting "hunt" for God in the visible world is found in his short but remarkably strange treatise *On the Three Days*. Hugh begins by talking about the natural world as a text that reveals God to those who know how to read it:

> This world is a sensible book that has divinity written into it. Individual creatures are letters and reveal some aspect of divinity. For the immensity of the world reveals divine power; the beauty of the world, divine wisdom; and the utility of the world, divine goodness. (*Three Days* 4.3)[28]

Hugh goes on to show how studying these natural "traces" lifts the mind up to God. By paying attention to the "magnitude" and "multitude" of the world, we can find examples of God's power. By paying attention to the world's beauty and abundance, we can get a taste for the order and benignity of God. In other words, as Hugh zooms in to focus on the properties of the natural world, he finds, as he thinks, traces of the Trinity in the natural world. For example, when commenting on the evidence of God's power in the world, Hugh draws attention to the diversity of shapes and variety of patterns (*Three Days* 2.2). What follows are pages and pages devoted to cataloging all the kinds of creatures, their shapes, and their composition. Hugh enumerates "the mass of mountains, the courses of rivers, the spaces of fields, the height of heaven, and the depth of the abyss" as examples (*Three Days* 3.1). Later, he argues that the beauty of the world can also be found in extraordinary shapes, in the variety of color, in that which is huge, tiny, unusual, particularly beautiful, or even monstrous. All these things cause us to marvel: giants among men, whales among fish, gryphons among birds, elephants among quadrupeds, dragons among serpents (*Three Days* 9.2). But in what is perhaps the most moving part of the treatise, Hugh attempts to illustrate how immensity can be found in the world by providing lengthy lists of examples of magnitude, multitude, and gratuitous beauty. The treatise takes on a dizzying tone as Hugh continues to heap up

enthusiastically example after example, eulogizing the abundance
of things in the universe:

> O how many things! How many there are! Count the stars of
> heaven, the sands of the sea, the dust of the earth, the drops of rain,
> the feathers of birds, the scales of fish, the hairs of animals, the
> grasses in fields, the leaves and fruits of trees, and the innumerable
> number of innumerable other things! (*Three Days* 2.2)

When we take in the world comprehensively, we are stupefied
by its grandeur and sheer diversity and impressed by the Creator's
power in the traces of its *multitude* and *magnitude*, thus illustrat-
ing one of the central tenets of Hugh's teaching: "The truth of
invisible realities is figured forth through visible things."[29] Hugh's
natural contemplation leads us to a sense of prayerful gratitude
for the benignity of the Creator: God is too good, too benign,
too loving toward us.

Francis of Assisi and the Song of Creation

When it comes to that most cliché-ridden saint of the entire medieval period, Francis of Assisi (1181/82–1226), we have to be
prepared for a shock when we read about him in the "autho-
rized" biography, Saint Bonaventure's *Life of St. Francis*. Go to
Assisi, Italy, and wander around the wonderfully cramped medieval streets, and you'll see how we prefer to remember Francis
in our day: everywhere you'll find sentimental, softly airbrushed
pastel pictures of a man with a big toothy smile sweetly nuzzling
a baby lamb.

Bonaventure's Francis is different. To begin with, Bonaventure
(1221–1274) portrays a man who is not primarily concerned with
being nice. Francis is a seraphic mystic, a visionary, whose heart
burns with ardor for invisible things. As Bonaventure puts it, the
purpose of his life was "to ascend in an orderly progression from
the sensible realm to the intelligible, from the lesser to the greater"

(*LSF* II.8, 197).[30] Readers will recognize that, within the Platonic and Dionysian tradition, this is a loaded phrase; and Bonaventure, who was yet another author of a commentary on Dionysius, was tuned into it. In his *Journey of the Mind into God*, he had written an instruction manual about how to make such an intellectual ascent "through visible things to the invisible things"—a kind of new Christian "ladder of love."[31] So we shouldn't be surprised to find this mystical theme in the *Life of St. Francis* as well.

But a second surprise has to do with how Francis, according to Bonaventure, achieved such an intellectual ascent: he did it, paradoxically, by practicing extreme literalism regarding Scripture. When Francis had "not yet learned how to contemplate the things of heaven nor had he acquired a taste for the things of God" (*LSF* I.2, 187), he acted as if what was written in the Gospel was directed quite literally to him: "Through this the man of God understood as addressed to himself the Gospel text: *If you wish to come after me, deny yourself and take up your cross and follow me* (Matt. 16:24)" (*LSF* I.4, 189).

And so Francis, in imitation of Christ, went out into "solitary places, well suited for sorrow; and there he prayed incessantly with *unutterable groanings* (Rom. 8:26)" (*LSF* I.5, 189). Remembering Christ's injunction to give away your cloak (Matt. 5:40), Francis literally "took off his own garments and clothed" a man he met "on the spot" (*LSF* I.2, 187). Francis read Jesus's parable about the "pearl of great price" (Matt. 13:45–46), and, again in literal obedience, he decided that "to be a spiritual merchant one must begin with contempt for the world" (*LSF* I.4, 188), and he began to give away his father's wares! Reading in the book of Isaiah that Christ was "despised and rejected" (Isa. 53:3), Francis, at first repulsed by the fact that their skin was falling off their bodies, overcame his disgust and began not just to tend to lepers but to kiss their sores (*LSF* I.5–6). And reading about how Christ was an outcast and had no beauty, he found himself swapping clothes with homeless beggars out of his desire to conform literally to the life of Christ ("so that he might carry externally in his body the cross of Christ," *LSF* I.6, 190). Ironically, though, through such severe literalism Francis began to have breakthrough moments in which he possessed metaphorical and spiritual realities. When he wore shabby clothes, he clothed himself in the humility of Christ. When he skipped multiple meals, he began to hunger for Christ. In this way he was given power "in interpreting divine mysteries" and learned how to "pass through visible images to grasp the invisible truth beyond" (*LSF* I.3, 188).

All of this literalism and treating the Bible as if it were directly addressing *him* led Francis, if it can be believed, to an *askesis* even more severe than that practiced in the monasteries (see *LSF* V). For those of us accustomed to thinking of Francis as a softy, Bonaventure's sternness is bracing. Francis was "unbending in . . . discipline. . . . Around the beginning of his conversion, in wintertime he often plunged into a ditch full of icy water in order to perfectly subjugate the enemy within" (*LSF* V.3, 220). "For many years [he] never tasted bread or wine" (IV.8, 213); he was often "fatigued from . . . prolonged activity and feeling hungry," and yet he would not "turn back from the promise [he] had made to holy poverty, in spite of any pressure from lack of food or other trials" (IV.1, 207); he trained himself to kiss the sores of lepers (I.5–6).

But Bonaventure constantly records irruptions of joy in the midst of such extreme acts of self-abnegation and voluntary poverty. The pope, who initially hesitated to approve the *Rule* of this strange-smelling but devout man, was won over when he saw "in the man of God such remarkable purity and simplicity of heart, such firmness of purpose and such fiery ardor of will" (*LSF* III.9, 205). Or: "Fatigued from their prolonged activity and feeling hungry, they stopped at an isolated spot. When there seemed to be no way for them to get the food they needed, God's providence immediately came to their aid. For suddenly a man appeared carrying bread. . . . From this the poor friars . . . were refreshed more by the gift of God's generosity than by the food they had received for their bodies" (IV.1, 207). Or: "Then he dressed in the poor man's rags and spent that day in the midst of the poor with an unaccustomed joy of spirit" (I.5–6, 190). Or, when Francis was attacked, beaten up, and robbed by thieves, he responded in this way: "When they went away, he jumped out of the ditch, and brimming over with joy, in a loud voice began to make the forest resound with the praises of the Creator of all" (II.5, 195).

Throughout the *Life* we hear again and again about Francis's ardor, the fire of his heart, and about the splendor of the visions he saw. The *Life* is full of color words and brilliance, words for heat and light and flame. No wonder, then, that the paintings that were commissioned for the first medieval Franciscan churches have such visual clarity! The compositions of these frescoes are less cluttered than the paintings of the previous century: there are fewer random buildings; smaller, more meaningful figures to represent the sacred scene; and mountainous landscapes that really could be Umbria. And the new technique of linear perspective begins to show up. This painterly revolution seems to have its roots in the Franciscan desire to create images that move viewers on the *literal* level—that is, images that touch the heart and cause it to burn with fire: "Many people also, not only stirred by devotion but inflamed by a desire for the perfection of Christ, despised the emptiness of worldly things and followed in the footsteps of Francis" (*LSF* IV.7, 211). And so we find in the church paintings of Umbria those experimental colors of the early Renaissance (blue, green, yellow, and pink!) and new orderly composition (the brilliant use of geometrical forms): when the crowded and the cluttered is stripped away, the underlying shapes come to the surface, now in efflorescent color; characters gesture, vigorously, in expression of their heartfelt affection. Giotto is the best commentator on Bonaventure's *Life*.

When we think about Bonaventure's *Life of St. Francis* in contrast to the background of Benedictine asceticism, we recognize that what is extraordinary about the Franciscan revolution is that natural contemplation plays such a crucial role in *this* life. It's not an eschatological end, but it has become part of the preliminary stage of the life of the spirit! *Praktike* and natural contemplation have been mapped on top of each other, and there is a direct, pro-portional relationship between my ability to hear the fullness of creation and my ability to disentangle my grasping fingers from its throat. Natural contemplation is back, but it is also pouring through the cracks of *askesis*, coming through the seams of the natural world, so that we get a glimpse of its deep colors just beneath the surface, like some old, faded medieval painting that must have been glorious in its original splendor. Francis, who longed to be totally transformed into God "by the fire of ecstatic love," was a man of "fervent charity which burned within [him]. . . . Like a glowing coal, he seemed totally absorbed in the flame of divine love" (*LSF* IX.1, 262).

Thus, when Francis achieved this level of love by means of the disciplined practices described above, he was able to hear the sym-phony of creation. Bonaventure explains: "Aroused by all things to the love of God, he *rejoiced* in all *the works of the Lord's hands* and from these joy-producing manifestations he rose to their life-giving principle and cause. In beautiful things he saw Beauty itself and through his *vestiges* imprinted on creation *he followed his Beloved* everywhere, making from all things a ladder by which he could climb up and embrace him *who is utterly desirable*. With a feeling of unprecedented devotion he savored in each and every creature—as in so many rivulets—that Goodness which is their fountain-source" (*LSF* IX.1, 262). This is the ascetic context for Francis's famous "Canticle of Brother Sun," written in his native Umbrian dialect—that is, without any traces of a self-satisfied high culture, but in the rough native accent of a local:

> Most high, all-powerful, all good, Lord!
> All praise is yours, all glory, all honor
> And all blessing.

> All praise be yours, my Lord, through all that you have
>   made,
> And first my lord Brother Sun,
> Who brings the day; and light you give us through him.

How beautiful is he, how radiant in all his splendour!
Of you, Most High, he bears the likeness.

All praise be yours, my Lord, through Sister Moon and
   Stars;
In the heavens you have made them, bright
And precious and fair.

All praise be yours, my Lord, through Brothers Wind
   and Air,
And fair and stormy, all the weather's moods,
By which you cherish all that you have made.

All praise be yours, my Lord, through Sister Water,
So useful, lowly, precious and pure.

All praise be yours, my Lord, through Brother Fire,
Through whom you brighten up the night.
How beautiful is he, how gay! Full of power and
   strength.

All praise be yours, my Lord, through Sister Earth, our
   mother,
Who feeds us in her sovereignty and produces
Various fruits with coloured flowers and herbs.[32]

For Francis, this is a hard-won vision, but when we have it, we
have enlarged our own being by allowing the prayer of the universe
to become our prayer as well. The natural creation waits in mute
silence to be performed through prayer in my heart, like a score
groaning for a musician to play it.

Angela of Foligno: The Empty Self

I conclude this chapter by briefly discussing an extraordinary Franciscan mystic, Angela of Foligno (1248–1309), who both carried
on the Franciscan tradition of the "literal" imitation of Christ
and Scripture and combined such literalism with the teaching on

darkness found in Dionysius the Areopagite. Doing so created an intense, moving, and at times grisly story of repentance, penance, suffering, abandonment, and visions. Her story was written in collaboration with a Franciscan brother, and it is called the *Memorial*.[33] Her teachings (*Instructions*) for the laity and third-order Franciscans make up the second part of what is known as *The Book of the Blessed Angela of Foligno*.

Angela, not unlike Francis, had the "perfect life"; she was born into a well-off family in thirteenth-century Umbria (Foligno is just down the road from Assisi, in the Vale of Spoleto). But she began experiencing a strange, inner discontent. At first, she tells us in the story of her conversion, she was hampered by familial expectations from responding to these inner calls to live more radically. She perceived so much resistance to her new desire to love God with no reserve that she even made superficial confessions, hiding from herself and God her true, inner state. But when the rest of her family died within a short period of time, she was left alone and thus able to put into place her plan for a complete, radical, and full dedication to the love of God. She began by dedicating each part of her body to God, member by member (*Mem.* I, 126). This was the start of her incredible journey of stripping away everything from her life but the love of God. We can hear echoes of Francis's love of "holy poverty."

In broad outline, the three main phases of *physike*, *theoria*, and *theologia* (or purification, illumination, and union) are still here, but Angela lets these phases uncoil into an incredible initial twenty steps that are followed by seven supplementary steps for those advanced in the spiritual life. The first twenty steps are largely concerned with asceticism, here slightly reimagined to be more in tune with cleansing and enkindling the affections of the heart (see chap. 6, on affective spirituality, below). Step 1 is developing an awareness of one's sinfulness; step 2 is confession of sins. Then follow penance (step 3), growing awareness of divine mercy (step 4), knowledge of self (step 5), an illumination in which the soul is graced with an even deeper awareness of sin (step 6), meditatively looking at the cross (step 7), coming to feel that I am personally responsible for killing Jesus on the cross (step 8), imaginatively standing at the foot of the cross (step 9), and contemplating the wounds of Christ (step 10).

These steps are followed by ten more steps that combine an ever deeper compunction concerning sin, an ever deeper affective bond with the passion of Jesus, and an ever deeper desire to give up everything except the love of Jesus. Angela describes this as a desire for martyrdom—that is, as a desire to participate in a painful death in order to draw closer to the experience of Christ (*Mem.* I, 128). The negative steps of mourning and penance, though, slowly become mingled with positive movements in the soul in which the radical, penetrating presence of God suffuses the soul (although the sense of unworthiness and need for penance never entirely disappears). For instance, in step 18, Angela says that she had come so close to God that she couldn't help but let out a scream of affirmation anytime someone said something worthy of the Lord's love: "Afterward, this fire of the love of God in my heart became so intense that if I heard anyone speak about God I would scream. . . . Also, whenever I saw the passion of Christ depicted, I could hardly bear it, and I would come down with a fever and fall sick" (*Mem.* I, 131).

But it is only in the advanced or supplementary steps, after much emotional grief and physical deprivation, that the deep consolations of God's presence begin to flow through Angela's soul. During an experience of praying the Our Father, Angela hears a voice that says, "You are full of God," with the result that she "truly felt all the members of my body filled with the delights of God" (*Mem.* IV, 148). But in addition to these lessons, Angela also is made to see how God is present in the sacraments and how every soul is called to give the only thing it can, love (IV, 153). She learns that divine providence is beyond the reach of the human intellect because it is so generous (V, 167). In short, in these advanced stages Angela is made to see, piece by piece, that the world is "pregnant with God." According to her "cowriter," Angela had this experience while taking Communion:

> And immediately the eyes of my soul were opened, and in a vision I beheld the fullness of God in which I beheld and comprehended the whole of creation, that is, what is on this side and what is beyond the sea, the abyss, the sea itself, and everything else. And in everything that I saw, I could perceive nothing except the presence of the power of God, and in a manner totally indescribable. And my soul in an excess of wonder cried out: "This world is pregnant with God!" Wherefore I understood how small is the whole of creation—that is, what is on this side and what is beyond the sea, the abyss, the sea itself, and everything else—but the power of God fills it all to overflowing. (*Mem.* VI, 169–70)

Throughout her *Memorial*, then, Angela tells the Franciscan story of how she responded to her desire to join herself to Christ by divesting herself of land, ornaments of beauty, and finery (*Mem.* I, 126), and of how this emptying of self led to an infilling of God. But the culmination comes toward the end of the book, where Angela describes how she was given a vision of the radical poverty of Christ, abandoned, alone, and despondent on the cross:

> Once I was meditating on the poverty of the Son of God incarnate. I saw his poverty—its greatness was demonstrated to my heart, to the extent that he wished me to see it—and I saw those for whom he had made himself poor. I then experienced such sorrow and remorse that I almost fainted. God wanted to demonstrate to me even more of his poverty. And I saw him poor of friends and relatives. I even saw him poor of himself and so poor that he seemed powerless to help himself. (*Mem.* VII, 179)

What she had not anticipated, though, is that, in her sixth supplementary step, she too would have to go through a period of divine abandonment, a time of mystical dereliction, in order to conform perfectly to the life of Christ. Angela went through a period of sickness in which she suffered every kind of bodily ailment along with a loss of her desire for virtue and a return of her vicious inclinations. Angela "found herself incapable of finding any other comparison than that of a man hanged by the neck who, with his hands tied behind him and his eyes blindfolded, remains dangling on the gallows and yet lives, with no help, no support, no remedy, swinging in the empty air. She added that the demons pushed her to despair even more cruelly than this" (*Mem.* VIII, 197). Brother Scribe adds, only a little reassuringly, "This sixth step, however, lasted but a short while, that is, about two years" (*Mem.* VIII, 199). Not surprisingly, Angela was brought to the breaking point: "There are even times when I am so overwhelmed with rage that I can hardly refrain from tearing myself apart. . . . When my soul sees all its virtues fall and leave, then it is overcome with fear and grief. It wails and cries out to God repeatedly and unceasingly: 'My son, my son, do not abandon me, my son!'" (*Mem.* VIII, 197–98). In other words, Angela, in living out the life of Christ in her own experience, utters to Jesus the words that Jesus had groaned to God the Father. She feels abandoned by God, like Christ on Good Friday.

The result of this excruciating experience was intellectual preparation for a vision of "darkness" that surpassed anything and everything she had seen before (*Mem.* VIII, 199). As Ariel Glucklich puts it, "Metaphorically, pain creates an embodied 'absence' and makes way for a new and greater 'presence.'"[34] Nothing but this abnegation of all comfort and consolation, Angela's own personal moment of divine abandonment, could have prepared her for the consummation of her spiritual ascent in which she saw God "in a darkness, and in a darkness precisely because the good that he is, is far too great to be conceived or understood. Indeed, anything conceivable or understandable does not attain this good or even come near it" (*Mem.* IX, 202). This darkness, like that described by Dionysius, is not an absence of joy but a supersaturation of perfection—so much so that it is blinding because it is an excess of light: "My soul has just been elevated to a state of joy so great that it is totally unspeakable. I cannot say anything about it. In this state I knew everything I wanted to know and possessed all I wanted to possess. I saw the All Good. . . . Henceforth, there is no good which could be described or even conceived in which I can place my hope. My hope rather lies in this secret good, one most certain and hidden that I understand is accompanied with such darkness" (*Mem.* IX, 203). Angela, as it turns out, is also a master of darkness. In her remarkable account leading up to this seventh supplementary step, she combines the Dionysian apophatic element of darkness with the Franciscan insistence on encountering God in my nerves, in my heart, and in the daily events of my life.

6

How to Perform Scripture

Lectio Divina and the Renewal of the Heart

Throughout Christian history, reading Scripture has been undertaken not just for gathering doctrines but also, and perhaps more often, for renewing the heart. You could say that, rather than just being studied, Scripture has been "performed." Ancient and medieval Christians in particular were alarmed by the great chasm between one's intellectual conviction that there is a God and one's actual ability to love him. As Augustine put it, once he was convinced of the truth of Christianity, he needed steadfastness more than certainty.[1] Our heads may be in the right place, but our hearts are not; or, to put it more accurately in terms of medieval terminology, love (*affectus*) has not been kindled in our hearts. But closing the gap between head knowledge and heart knowledge is a long, slow, and difficult process, one that takes time and repetition, in part because we spend a massive amount of time rationalizing our negative moral dispositions.

In the medieval period, the primary task taken up by monasticism was to develop a practice to bring about deep transformation—

to overcome the gap between head knowledge and heart knowledge. Monastic writers (such as those we will look at in this chapter) specialized in constructing exercises and meditations that led to this deep transformation, exercises through which souls became capable over time of not just assenting to truth but loving it, desiring it, responding with the whole heart. These exercises were like personal trainers for the soul. Writing in the twelfth century, Peter of Celle (1115–1183) describes such monastic discipline: "The true religious voluntarily and freely desires regular discipline in order to be tied back from the appetites of the flesh as if by bands. The bonds of religion are the regular statutes: for example, silence, fasting, and seclusion of the cloister, ways of acting which do not attract attention, compassion and fraternal love, paternal reverence, reading and persistent prayer, recollection of past evils, fear of death, the fire of purgatory, eternal fire."[2]

In the previous chapter we considered some of these spiritual exercises in relation to the desert fathers and Benedictine monasticism. However, over the centuries, one practice began to take pride of place among the repertoire of spiritual exercises: *lectio divina*, or a slow, heartfelt reading and absorption of Scripture.[3] In this chapter, then, I want to analyze how a few medieval texts—especially those written in the Carthusian tradition—talked about and practiced *lectio divina*. In particular, in what follows I will make reference to Guigo II's *The Ladder of Monks* (*Scala Claustralium*) and Hugh of Balma's *The Roads to Zion Mourn*, known in the Middle Ages simply as the *Via Purgativa*. But before I come to these texts, I want to put such spiritual reading in the context of medieval affective spirituality. That is, if Christianity had for centuries prayerfully approached Scripture believing that, through careful meditation, one can feed on the Word of God and digest it, late medieval variations on this ancient practice were particularly focused on the role of the heart in such reading—what has come to be known as affective spirituality.

Discovery of the Inner Landscape

It may be hard to imagine, but for most of Christian history—up to about the year 1000—the most important image of Christ was not of the man suffering on a cross but of a potent, Zeus-like divinity seated on a jewel-encrusted throne, like a supernatural Byzantine emperor. You can find this image, Christ Pantocrator ("Christ, Ruler of All"), in the apses of Byzantine churches (such as those in Greece, but also in Venice and Ravenna), but you can also find such a Christ on the tympana over the portals of Romanesque cathedrals in northern Europe—say, at the Abbey of St. Pierre in Moissac, France (twelfth century). He raises his right hand, gripping a book on his lap with his left hand. Around him the twenty-four elders of the Apocalypse (the book of Revelation) squirm with admiration and terror. Here is one who enfolds the universe, emanating power, strength, and imperial splendor.[4]

A little over two hundred years later, though—that is, in the late Middle Ages—the images of Christ could hardly be more different. Rather than portraying Christ as regal, authoritative, and in control of the universe, these images—especially in northern Europe (modern-day Germany, Belgium, the Czech Republic, and the Netherlands)—feature a dramatic change in taste: Christ is depicted as a broken, vulnerable, impotent failure. Such images are known as *Andachtsbilder*, from the German for "devotion" (*Andacht*) and "image" (*Bild*). Some of them are heartrendingly powerful, forcing us to confront a man of sorrows who has been stripped of all beauty and broken. Perhaps there has never been an image of Christ more powerful than Matthias Grünewald's Isenheim Altarpiece, which gives us a Christ screaming out in excruciating pain, while suffering from a terrible skin ailment.[5]

For many years, scholars have pointed out that this change in visual images of Christ paralleled a change in devotional texts, in a larger historical movement that has been termed the European "discovery of the self." As Caroline Walker Bynum puts it, "Interest in the inner landscape of the human being increases after

1050 in comparison to the immediately preceding period."[6] This was the age of Anselm, Bernard of Clairvaux, Hugh of St. Victor, Richard of St. Victor, the early Carthusians, and the Franciscans. The Carthusian Guigo I (1083–1136) wrote, "See how ignorant you are of your own self; there is no land so distant or so unknown to you, nor one about which you will so easily believe falsehoods."[7] Roughly contemporaneous to Guigo, Anselm (1034–1109) wrote,

> And now, man, flee, for a little while, the earthly occupations; take yourself away, for a while, from the tumultuous and disturbing thoughts; throw down now your burdensome cares, and put off your laborious tasks. Empty yourself for a bit before God, and rest for a while in him. Enter into the inner chamber of your mind, and keep out all things except God, and those things that will help you seek him out. And when the door is closed, seek after him; say now, with all my heart, say now to him: "I seek your face; your face, O Lord, I am seeking out!"[8]

In contrast, then, to the focus on communal order and military-like discipline in Benedict's *Rule*, or the focus on retreat from the world and the practice of ascetic discipline in Evagrius's *On Prayer*, this new, intimate, whispering, quiet, interior subjectivity—even if not entirely new to Christianity—swept in like a great wave and brought all kinds of popular piety (images, prayers, poems, songs, devotionals) along with it. If an earlier age had emphasized gaining tranquility of mind so that the intellect, unimpaired by the passions, can see clearly, the late medieval "discovery" of the inner and mysterious continent of the human *heart*—and all of its emotions and loves and fears and guilt—meant that methods and strategies were developed according to which the *interior homo* ("inner man") could be made known and cultivated.

One of the most interesting effects of the new "interest in the inner landscape of the human being" was how it affected the reading of Scripture. Although reading and commenting on and praying through the Scriptures had been an essential practice in

Christian devotion since the foundation of Christianity, the reading of Scripture was now drawn into this new emotional climate of affective spirituality, this European-wide phenomenon that constituted such an important chapter in the history of emotions.[9] Writers in this age are not only particularly concerned with the affections of the heart; they are also especially systematic in their method for reading Scripture for the purpose of prayer. Thus, a great age of *lectio divina* was born. *Lectio divina* was and is a kind of fluid reading activity that creates a spiritual space in which interior transformation may take place. You read, pause, think, sigh, and start to pray, before reading again. As Duncan Robertson has put it, *lectio divina* was a "movement of reading into prayer."[10] For this reason, monastic writers in the High Middle Ages felt that *lectio divina* was probably the single most important tool that serious Christians had at their disposal.

Cogitatio cordis mei (The Secret Thoughts of the Heart)[11]

The brevity and systematic nature of Guigo II's *Ladder of Monks* (or *Scala Claustralium*) were two of the most important factors that led to its extraordinarily widespread influence on European piety.[12] The ninth abbot of the monastery of the Grande Chartreuse—where the award-winning film *Into Great Silence* was shot—explains succinctly (nine pages in a modern edition) how *lectio divina* finds its consummation in the "experience" of God. Like many of his contemporaries, Guigo (1114–1193) describes the experience of God in exuberantly sensual terms: to experience God is to have desire inflamed, to be enveloped in the sweet dew of heaven, to be anointed with oil, to have hunger sated, to be made to forget earthly things, to be enlivened, and to be made drunk while still remaining sober (*Ladder* 5).[13] In fact, it is this experience that distinguishes true Christians from "secular philosophers." Both the secular philosopher and the Christian are able to use deep intellectual powers such as reasoning and meditation (*cogitatio* and *meditatio*), but secular philosophers lack what Guigo calls "the spirit of wisdom" (*spiritus sapientiae*), in which, if you have it, you can smell, taste, feel, and be warmed by the experience of God.

Guigo outlines a four-step reading process (a ladder with four rungs, a kind of rational schematization of Jacob's ladder in Gen. 28) that leads from the mere "letter of the word" to the experience of God. In other words, if for Plotinus and Augustine and Dionysius and Eckhart the mystical ascent was a dialectical exercise of the intellect, and for Evagrius and Cassian and Francis it was a muscular practice of the will through *askesis*, for Guigo and other Carthusians the ladder of ascent is found within the very exercise of "performing" Scripture with the heart.

The first rung of the ladder is what Guigo calls *lectio*, an attentive reading of Scripture with an alert expectation that the words under consideration are "sweet and crammed full of meaning" (*Ladder* 1). *Meditatio* (meditation), the second rung, seeks out fuller explanation, allowing the mind to play freely over the face of Scripture. Guigo illustrates *meditatio* with reference to Matthew 5:8, "Blessed are the pure in heart: for they shall see God." The mind first considers the words one at a time, locating each one in a network of related terms. The mind recalls, for instance, how Psalm 24:4 says that only those who have clean hands and a pure heart will ascend to God; or how the psalmist prayed, "Create in me a clean heart" (Ps. 51:10); or how Job "made a covenant" with his eyes (Job 31:1). The mind then considers the final part of Matthew 5:8, asking in what way the *visio Dei* will satisfy all desires (*Ladder* 2). Guigo continues, though, by saying that this meditation on the greatness of the promise of a vision of God leads to a confrontation with the weakness of my soul—that is, my limpid will. Faced with the disheartening contrast between the greatness of the vision and the soul's weakness, I am ushered into an impassioned state of panting, thirsting, and longing for heavenly things. On this rung, known as *oratio*, the soul begins to long to know God, no longer in a superficial way (according to the "letter") but in the sense of experience (*Ladder 5*). And finally, while I am in this state of prayer, it sometimes happens that "increased desire" comes and "fire is ignited" within (*Ladder 5*). In short, the process of meditating on scriptural words leads to a state of longing where speech comes to an end. In prayer, "desire is inflamed" and "the soul's *affectus* is stretched out broad" (*Ladder 5*). *Oratio* (prayer), then, finds its affective consummation in the final stage of *contemplatio* (contemplation) (*Ladder 6*).

It's helpful to compare Guigo's *Ladder of Monks* to another text by a Carthusian writer known as Hugh of Balma (d. 1439), whose *The Roads to Zion Mourn* was also massively influential. In Hugh we find a particularly masterful and well-thought-out example of how to "perform" scriptural reading with the heart.

At the beginning of *The Roads to Zion Mourn*, Hugh takes aim at writers who treat the essence of Christianity to be that of holding correct doctrines: "In our day and age, many religious, indeed, many well-known and respected men, have abandoned the true wisdom in which God alone is worshiped perfectly. . . . They wretchedly fill themselves with all sorts of knowledge, as if to fabricate idols for themselves out of various newfound proofs. . . . For God did not intend that the soul he created should be stuffed so full of sheepskin copybooks that his goodness is pushed aside" (*Zion* 1–2, 69).[14] Rather, the highest reaches of Christianity are achieved only by "the same wisdom that stretches toward God by love's longing. As far as the east is from the west, so incomparably does mystical wisdom excel all created knowledge" (*Zion* 2, 69–70). For Hugh, then, given that "the human spirit can learn this wisdom only from God directly," what we need is to clear a space within the heart where we may be "affected into God" (*Zion* 6, 70). That is, we must follow a rational and moral path of cleansing and enlightenment that will lead us to the point where "the *affectus*, disposed by love and transcending all human understanding, soars above. . . . This, therefore, is *mystical theology*, that is, the hidden divine word with which the human spirit, disposed by ardor of

love, converses secretly with Christ her Beloved in the language
of the affections" (*Zion* 7, 71).

As with Guigo, "the affections" are not the same as emotions:
you can't just program them to feel warm or enthusiastic. Rather,
they are a kind of inner, spiritual knowing, a drawing-near-to and
clinging (accompanied by a warmth of the heart) that brings about
a deep connection between the soul and God. It is a participation
in nothing less than the love of the seraphim, who know God by
loving him: "The third path, the unitive way, corresponds to the
Seraphim, a term meaning *glowing*. In this path the soul is carried into God with such great ardor that sometimes the body is
utterly and marvelously overwhelmed as the person's *affects* and
movements stretch out toward God" (*Zion* II.9, 84). But, again,
you can't just skip to this stage of deep affection. You have to go
through two lower stages of preparation. The first stage is that
of purgation; the second is the path of illumination, in which the
mind undergoes a series of disciplined meditational exercises on
Scripture. Only then do you get to the third level, the "unitive"
path, "in which the spirit [is] carried aloft by God alone" and "is
led beyond every reason, knowledge, and understanding" (*Zion*
5, 70).

For Hugh, the path of purgation is less one of severe ascetical
exercises (as it was for Evagrius, Cassian, and Angela of Foligno) or corporate discipline (as it was for Benedict) than it is
"affective"—that is, it is a path on which you come to regret deeply,
on the level of the heart, your past sins and distance from God.
And so the soul should "revisit her sins in some sort of hidden
place, especially in the hidden silence of the night" (*Zion* I.3, 75).
Enumerate ten or twelve of your main sins. Name them. Speak
them directly to God. And as you name them, sigh, exalt God, and
put your own soul as far down as you can. The soul should "sigh
and groan" as best she can: "Just as a file applied to iron pushes
away a bit of the iron's rust with each grating stroke, so too any
sort of sigh or groan removes something of the rust of sin" (*Zion*
I.3, 75). Then recall the nobility God gave you—how you are made

in the image of God. Reflect on the divine incarnation, and think about Christ's passion. This leads the soul to cry out, "What then should a wretch like me do, when I—the cause of your death—not only do not repay your goodness but instead further provoke you with my stinking misdeeds?" (*Zion* I.5, 76). In this way the soul mingles self-examination and regret with the praise of God, being careful not to become too verbose ("[Be] careful not to lapse into mere wordiness, let [the soul] pray these or similar phrases with growing affectedness," *Zion* I.11, 79). We can feel the influence of Guigo's *Ladder* and his emphasis on the "new" affective path. In a way that would have been difficult for Benedict to foresee, the affective life now has a place in the spiritual life.

At some point, my meditation on God's mercy begins to be enlarged significantly. As I contemplate God, I momentarily forget to worry about myself primarily, and I ask not just for my own forgiveness but for God to pour forth mercy onto the whole world. This is a profound moment in Hugh, analogous to the famous passage in Isaac the Syrian (quoted above) or Evagrius's idea of natural contemplation, but in a new affective key:

> Now, if the human spirit is to see her yearning fulfilled, she ought to take a cue from the manner in which God pours himself out. For the Spiritual Sun, Jerusalem the Heavenly City, spreads her rays of goodness over the good and the bad alike. So too the human spirit ought to implore the Creator from the bottom of her heart to extend his forgiveness to everyone bearing the image of the most Blessed Trinity, not just to herself or to those close to her. May the Creator redeem all those he has created, coming to their aid mercifully, regardless of what they deserve. . . . In some instances she may restrict her petition to prayers for herself and for specific others, yet charity is always spreading itself more widely, and, as far as she can, she ought to employ the same solicitously affective manner that she uses for herself in her prayers for everyone else. And so she should pray: "Good, Beautiful, Lord, Sweet, and Merciful, have mercy on all sinners, whom you have redeemed with your precious blood." And then, as far as possible, let her imagine, as

she says, "Have mercy," that the entire world is bowing in genuine
worship and fitting reverence toward its Creator. (*Zion* I.12, 79–80)

This is, you could say, the very top of stage 1—cleaning the mirror of my soul—but we can already see how this cultivation of
the spirit toward repentance is breaking into a higher stage, an
expansiveness of the heart.

And thus we climb higher. The second stage is mental exercise
or, as Hugh puts it, employing the anagogical method (a reading of Scripture with an "upward movement"), by which Hugh
means removing the "darkened outer husk" which refers to "sense-
perceptible creatures," thus allowing us to get at spiritual interiors.
Through this anagogical action I allow Scripture to write within
me what had been written on the page; but as it is translated from
written words into the content of my heart, it also becomes something new and "affected." In particular, Hugh takes the Song of
Songs as the great key signature in which all Scripture should be
read: "For these petitions [found in the Song of Songs] are nothing
other than inflamed yearnings and restless affections calling more
ardently on the Beloved so that the bride might more joyously
attain upwardness" (*Zion* II.12, 85). Once we have absorbed the
plaintive cries of the Song of Songs, we then can turn back to the
Gospels or Psalms or any other biblical book. We're now ready
to start reading affectively. What does this look like specifically?
Hugh illustrates his method with respect to the Our Father (or
Lord's Prayer).

Hugh takes the Our Father phrase by phrase, and sometimes
word by word, lingering over each bit, questioning it, and trying
to get it to release the fragrance of its pure essence. And so, when
we read "Our Father which art in heaven," we immediately pause.
Hugh breaks even this short phrase into three separate meditations: "In a literal sense *father* simply means the one who engenders a son. . . . Transferring this to the anagogic sense, someone
is most truly said to be a father when he engenders many sons
adoptively . . . from the seed of deifying love he has emitted"

(*Zion* II.14, 86). The mind takes the idea of "father" and expands it, as it were, to include not just paternal sires but also any life-donating force or movement. And then we remember that this generous paternal outpouring is modified by the word "our": we get to call God "our" father. He is not the special property of a religious elite, a being known only to a lofty priesthood, but in his radiance he draws "all rational spirits" to himself. In fact, "no human or angelic spirit can hide itself from [his] naturally attracting warmth" (*Zion* II.15, 87).

Next is "which art *in heaven.*" Hugh meditates on the nature of the heavens and points out that the stars above are steadfast, continuously in motion, and adorned with a variety of constellations. Hugh then briefly draws on the language of desire from the Song of Songs, dwelling on what it would be like to have such starlike constancy, such inner steadfastness. What would it be like to return to the root of our being and to remain there in desire? While remaining steadfast, could I also remain in "continuous movement" (again, akin to the heavens), as opposed to my usual "sluggish and laborious motion"? If so, could I allow God to become the "movement of love" within me? If I accomplished all that, then I could be—interiorly—in spiritual motion and in constancy simultaneously. I too could be adorned with a variety of "constellations." I could "sparkle with the splendor of virtues just as the heavens are resplendent with the constellations of stars" (*Zion* II.18, 89). What was written in scriptural words external to me has been rewritten within my heart by means of my affections.

As we can see, Hugh of Balma's way of reading Scripture unfolds in two movements. In the first movement, I take the words of Scripture and expand them or, rather, generalize them, abstract them from their particular references and relate them to some universal force or virtue or power behind them (e.g., "father" becomes a life-donating principle of care; "heavens" becomes that admirable state of steadfastness, dynamic movement, and splendor). After I have unfolded these specific references into more universal beauties, and after I have come to admire them within my

mind, to wonder at them in the eye of my imagination, the next
stage is to want them, to ask for them, to long for them—in other
words, to pine in affection for them. I want them inside me. I want
Scripture to write itself on my heart. I have moved into prayer.[15]

And something strange starts happening when I am in the state
of desire/prayer: I begin to have longings and groanings "too deep
for words," as Paul puts it (Rom. 8:26). Or, as Hugh says, "Then
the soul steps up to a much higher level, in which, as often as she
wishes, without any cogitation leading the way, she is directly
affected into God, something that cannot be taught by any sort
of human effort" (*Zion* 6, 71). For Hugh, this final stage is a
kind of combination of what Bernard had called "the kiss of the
mouth"[16] and how "that outstanding teacher, blessed Denis the
Areopagite, describes" wisdom (*Zion* III.2, 106). It is the moment
in which I am lifted up and receive a "down-payment on eternal
felicity" when my soul is "raised by extended practice of ardent
aspirations. For where she loves she lives, and the importunate
reach of her yearnings finds something of a natural end-point,
coming to rest in him toward whom she stretches herself" (*Zion*
III.6, 109). In this way, both "philosophy" (mental training) and
pious cultivation of the interior life lead up to a height that excels
both of them—to an "experience" (as Guigo puts it) in which we
are taught by the inner teacher:

> Thus, through practice in the cleansing and illuminative ways and
> under the inward instruction and direction of God alone, the soul
> learns experientially what no mortal science or eloquence can un-
> lock. For love alone teaches most inwardly what neither Aristotle
> nor Plato nor any other mortal philosophy or science ever could or
> ever can understand. This means that each rational soul can learn
> her knowledge from the loftiest and eternal Professor, knowledge
> in which all reason, knowledge, and understanding falls away, and
> the *affectus*, disposed by love and transcending all human under-
> standing, soars above, steering the spirit solely by the rule of unitive
> love toward him who is the source of all goodness. This, therefore,

is *mystical theology*, that is, the hidden divine word with which the human spirit, disposed by ardor of love, converses secretly with Christ her Beloved in the language of the affections. (*Zion* 7, 71)

Thus, in his scriptural meditation, Hugh's mind pivots back and forth from the text of the Lord's Prayer to the yearning and groaning of the Song of Songs. He uncovers first the "pure essence," as it were, of each phrase of the Our Father and then flips back to the Song to inspire a petitionary spirit within the soul. In this way the soul can uncover a "ray of light," a moment of anagogy in any scriptural passage, because "this ray of light lies hidden beneath Scripture" (*Zion* II.8, 83). By applying this method to the Psalms or the Gospels or any other biblical book, the soul "clears the way to carry anagogic affections to the Beloved . . . so that through guiding cogitation a bit of a spark in the spirit might begin to affect her toward [God]" (*Zion* II.45, 103). But in the final state of the soul, all such meditation and cogitation will be left behind.

Eckhart: Virtuoso Performer of Scripture

Throughout this chapter, in order to describe this prayerful, medieval practice of reading Scripture (*lectio divina*), I've used the metaphor of *performing* Scripture. And I've focused on two great Carthusian masters who specialized in "affecting" the soul into God. In this final section, I conclude by looking at a virtuoso reader of Scripture, Meister Eckhart, who "performs" biblical truth in his homilies like some kind of Paganini or Rachmaninoff of Scripture, as strange as this may sound.

As modern, "scientific" readers, we read a passage of Scripture to find out what it means—that is, what it meant to the original author. But Eckhart believed that any given scriptural passage could have dozens of meanings, a whole semantic range of correct meanings. For Eckhart, as for his medieval contemporaries, the more fundamental distinction was between "outer" readings and an "inner" meaning. The surface level of the biblical text speaks "excessively" or "superabundantly"; thus, Eckhart in his homilies—publicly performed acts of *lectio divina*—could look at each word of a passage in turn and spin a web of intertextuality, connecting them to dozens of other parts of Scripture. But what he is really interested in is, in a phrase that echoes Guigo II, what lies beneath the shell; that is, he wants to cause a "breakthrough" in which the mind gets through the outer shell of the text into its inner meaning. That deep inner meaning is achieved when the reader experiences the "birth of the Word"—that is, when he can begin to see "all things from the divine perspective, the 'now' (*nû/nunc*) of eternity in which all words and expressions are one in the eternal Word."[17]

The particular sermon I want to focus on is the German sermon in which Eckhart preaches on the Gospel text "Jesus entered into the temple and began to throw out those who were selling and buying" ("Intravit Jesus in templum," Matt. 21:12).[18] Perhaps not surprisingly, Eckhart allegorizes the passage, suggesting that the "temple" here represents the "soul"; "that is why God wishes the temple to be empty, so that there shall be nothing there but himself" (Sermon 12, 152). But almost immediately after that, Eckhart destabilizes our reading of the passage with an unexpected reading of who the sellers and buyers are. We might expect to hear that they represent the vice of avarice within the human soul, but Eckhart interprets them as good people who clutter up the soul with pious deeds—specifically, as those who think that God primarily wants us "to be good," that the essence of the religious life is morality, and that he will reward us if we follow his rules. Fully aware of how surprising his words are, Eckhart explains that the sellers and buyers are indeed good people. They refrain from serious sin. They want to be good. They take on fasting, keep vigils, and pray—and yet, all the good works they do, they perform "in order that our Lord should give them something in return." They are "merchants" who want to barter with God (Sermon 12, 153). Such people think that by doing pious things they put God under an obligation and that he will reward them, but God, who needs nothing, is completely free of such obligations: "God does not seek his own interests but in all his works he is untrammelled and free and acts from pure love" (Sermon 12, 154).

In Eckhart's conception, God is a little like one of those moments we rarely let ourselves enjoy, one in which we are caught up dancing to some absurd song, knowing it's absurd and yet not caring if anyone else thinks so. Caught up in our own enjoyment, we don't need or want anything. If someone approaches us with some matter of business or a philosophical question, we are completely unmoved because what we have at present is more vital than some matter of propriety. Such an analogy may seem a bit too homespun, but it wasn't for Eckhart. In another sermon, Eckhart talks about God's laughter. The least good deed done with the least amount of genuine goodwill causes "all the saints in heaven and earth and all the angels rejoice with such great joy as all the joys of this world cannot equal. And the higher each saint is the greater his joy, and the higher each angel is the greater his joy, and yet all their joy combined is as small as a lentil compared with the joy that God has at that act. For God makes merry and laughs at good deeds" ("Laudate Coeli," Sermon 91, 445). And in yet another sermon, Eckhart, in a way reminiscent of Gerard Manley Hopkins, talks about God at play. According to Eckhart, God delights in those things which are like himself, "just as if one were to turn a horse loose in a green meadow that was entirely smooth and level, and it would be the horse's nature to let himself go with all his strength in galloping about the meadow—he would enjoy it for it is his nature" ("Qui audit me non confundetur," Sermon 57, 297).

Thus, when we go back and think about our merchant of piety trying to barter with God, we see the futility of it. But if God doesn't chiefly or essentially want us to be good, what does he want? Eckhart's answer is equally disorienting: God wants us to be free, like him. Of all the things in the universe, Eckhart says, there is nothing more beautiful or magnificent than the human soul because it is most like God; and it is most Godlike when it participates in this almost giddy freedom (Sermon 12). This is an extraordinary thing to say.

Later in the same homily, Eckhart notes that, although he spoke gently to them, Christ chastised the sellers of doves, who represent those good people who perform good works not merely out of their own self-interest but nevertheless not yet out of that sense of freedom (Sermon 12). Eckhart adds, "This is how the doves can be removed, which means to say the obstacles and self-attachment of all those works which are otherwise good" (Sermon 12, 155). It is this extraordinary capacity for freedom, what Eckhart calls living "with neither a before nor an after," that we find when we "cleanse the temple" of the soul. When it is quiet, Jesus can speak within: "If Jesus is to speak in the soul, then she must be alone and must herself be silent if she is to hear Jesus" (Sermon 12, 156). When I have emptied myself of the clutter of dolorous piety, then God can pray to God within (Sermon 12).

This moment, which Eckhart refers to as God praying to God within (a kind of take on Paul's "Ye have received the Spirit of adoption, whereby we cry, Abba, Father," Rom. 8:15), is what scriptural *lectio* aims at. Eckhart is a master at digging deep into Scripture—not just pulling "truths" from it but getting at the ultimate truth underneath it all: God's invitation to us to be like him by means of falling into him. In yet another daring metaphor, Eckhart describes this breakthrough moment of scriptural reading with the potent metaphor of falling: "When the soul enters the light that is pure, she falls so far from her own created somethingness into her nothingness that in this nothingness she can no longer return to created somethingness by her own power. But God places himself with his uncreatedness beneath her nothingness and contains the soul in his somethingness. The soul has dared to become nothing and cannot return to herself by her own power—so far has she gone out of herself before God catches her" (Sermon 12, 156). Perhaps no experience is more disorienting than the sensation of free fall. It's one of two things (the other being loud noises) that human infants are naturally afraid of (hence their so-called Moro reflex). It's only later that a toddler, being tossed by her father, realizes that the feeling of falling can be playful. In Eckhart we find a similar mix of fearfulness and playfulness: we walk over a precipice in the dark and feel a total abandonment into nothingness. But in that fall we are, as it were, continually being caught. This is *like* what it means to live in total freedom. This is what it means to be *like* God. If I've achieved this, then pious deeds will come, but they will no longer be acts of bartering with God.

This, then, is the goal of Eckhart's preaching: to read Scripture not only to appreciate spiritual things (justice, charity, piety, and so on) but also to move even further in, "break through," and taste the "source" itself. It is for this reason that Bernard McGinn has called Eckhart an "apophatic exegete," citing Eckhart's own words: "I have said before, the shell must be broken through and what is inside must come out, for if you want to get at the kernel you must break the shell. And also, if you want to find nature unveiled, all likenesses must be broken through, and the further you penetrate, the nearer you will get to the essence. When the soul finds the One, where all is one, there she will remain in the Single One."[19]

Scholarship has much to say about the import of various theological terms and potential missteps in Eckhart's teachings, but we cannot forget the childlike giddiness of Eckhart himself. Reading Eckhart makes you feel like you've shed weight, become lighter and almost giddy. For us moderns, who have come to think of religion as, essentially, disciplined living, morality, and duty, Eckhart's words are almost ridiculous—in the truest sense, laughable. At the heart of Eckhart's vision of Christianity is an ocean of joy, with its kaleidoscopically refracted millions of colors shifting in their jewellike tones. For Eckhart and the Carthusians, reading Scripture in a meditative way, in which I try to drink in the burning words of God, is how I renew the heart and regain a vision of the wildness of scriptural promises.

Conclusion

The Wildness of the Spiritual Life

> I should call him blessed and holy to whom it is given to experience
> even for a single instant something which is rare indeed in this life.
> To lose yourself as though you did not exist and to have no sense
> of yourself, to be emptied out of yourself and almost annihilated,
> belongs to heavenly not to human love.
>
> —Bernard of Clairvaux, *On Loving God*

Throughout this book I have spoken a lot about our love *for* God. To conclude, I want to talk about the love *of* God—that is, God's love for us. The discussion of the "abyss" and "nothingness" and "darkness" of God in the preceding chapters might give readers the impression that God is impersonal, a kind of spiritual black hole or unfeeling force or cold Pythagorean paradigm. This vision of the One is found in Plato and Plotinus, as we have seen, and to a certain extent in Christian authors (such as Meister Eckhart) who venerated their memory and often repeated similar lofty and aloof formulas. But Christians, of course, believe in a God who has, as John Henry Newman put it, "personality."[1] Or in the words of Blaise Pascal, there's a great difference between "the God of the philosophers" and the God of the Christians.[2]

In particular, Christians hold two doctrines that distinguish the God of Abraham, Isaac, and Jacob from the Neoplatonic One. First, the Christian God made the world ex nihilo, as opposed to serving as its First Cause, an unconscious emanation of the world.[3] Second, the Christian God became incarnate in human flesh. For Augustine, the incarnation (and all that it implied) was the one thing he couldn't find in his beloved *libri Platonici* (*Conf.* VII). The doctrine of the incarnation implies a loving, self-giving God, and it calls for a corresponding stooping humility in us— that is, we must accept our inability to perfect our own return to God. The extraordinary thing about this God, then, in the words of contemporary theologian Janet Soskice, is his "kindness," by which she means God's desire to enter into "kinship" with us, to join us together with him in a "family."[4]

The doctrine of creation ex nihilo has similar implications. While the Platonists believed in a One who was unaware that the world existed, Christians believe in a God who made everything from nothing. What follows from this is of shattering importance: the God who makes is also the God who sustains, holds in being, and tenderly cares for the existential structure of creatures. For Christians, God's making cannot be separated from his continuing to make. If God dropped his attention toward the world, so to speak, then matter and time and space would evaporate. And so he is nearby; he sustains his creation. In other words, the story of the Christian God needs to account not only for our love for God (the mystical ascent that pulls us up and beyond reason into the fathomless region beyond "being") but also for the love of God and his providential, almost eager and giddy, concern for us.

Over the course of this book I have pivoted between emphasizing the positive, affective disposition toward God (as seen and felt so prominently in Augustine, Guigo II, and Hugh of Balma) and the negative (or apophatic) approach to God's transcendence (Dionysius and Eckhart, in particular). We might note that these different perspectives have reemerged as poles in contemporary theological discussions, as represented by two great contemporary French philosophers/theologians: Jean-Luc Marion and Emmanuel Falque. Marion's famous *God without Being* centers on the distinction between an idol and an icon, the difference being that an idol radically contents me and obliterates my sense of need, whereas an icon pulls me up through it into an infinitely receding horizon.[5] Falque, on the other hand, is interested in the opposite spiritual movement—not of the receding nature of being, which withdraws from our facile attempts to mentally manipulate it, but of a God who crowds into our time and space, trying to be as present as possible.[6] This is precisely the tension Karl Rahner emphasized: we have to hold before us a God who is both "without a name" and to whom we say "thou."[7]

I conclude this book by discussing four more medieval masters, two who describe not just our love for God but God's love for us (Bernard of Clairvaux and Julian of Norwich), and two (John Ruusbroec and Nicholas of Cusa) who managed to bring together the visions of a God of unfathomable depths into whom we fall as into an abyss *and* who is simultaneously rushing out, pursuing us, surrounding us, constantly invading time to sustain us, seek us, and be near, around, and in us. In other words, if we map these unique characteristics of the Christian God (his "personality" and providential "kindness") onto the God from classical antiquity (the One who is "beyond being"), we get a dazzling image of a God whose transcendence is found in his mind-boggling benignity—or as Ruusbroec put it, "the maelstrom of God's love" (*Sparkling Stone*, 158–59).

The "Kindness" of God: Bernard of Clairvaux and Julian of Norwich

In his treatise *On Loving God*, the twelfth-century preacher and monastic reformer Bernard of Clairvaux (1090–1153) lets his kaleidoscopic, associative memory mingle all kinds of powerful images to impress upon the soul the full weight of its blessedness. *On Loving God* is, we could say, a commentary on two well-known scriptural declarations: we love God because "he first loved us" (1 John 4:9–10) and "God so loved the world that he gave his only-begotten Son" (John 3:16) (*On Loving God* II.1). But Bernard helps us to see those well-worn passages not as clichés but as poignant and memorable assertions. For Bernard, our ordinary condition of ingratitude is exposed when we begin to think about "the innumerable kindnesses [God] showers on men for their benefit. . . . For who else provides food for everyone who eats, light for seeing, air to breathe? It would be foolish to want to list them when I have just said that they are innumerable" (II.2, 175).

When you read something like Cormac McCarthy's *The Road* and are led to imagine a world that has lost color, civility, clean air, vegetation, and friendship, then you recover the ability to see what gratuitous bounty we live in: the purity of air, the brilliance of light, warm bread, wine. There are also the "higher goods" in the higher parts of the human soul: dignity, knowledge, virtue, free will, courage, hunger for our Creator, the ability to care for the world, the ability and desire to worship (II.2). But surrounded by so many and such good blessings, we usually turn a blind eye of ingratitude to the world. Bernard gets a little carried away in proving this ("We have wandered too far from our subject," II.6, 178), but his point is that the world is pure giftedness: "To sum up what has been said: Is there anyone, even an unbeliever, who does not know that he has received the necessities of bodily life in this world—by means of which he survives, sees and breathes—from no other but him who gives food to all flesh, who causes his sun to rise on the good and wicked alike, and the rain to fall on the just and the unjust . . . [and who does not know] that human dignity which shines from his soul . . . [and who does not know] the gift of virtue?" (II.6, 178). And then there's the fact that God, who created, continually re-creates throughout history, saving people despite their sin, performing miracles, and calling back those who stray (VI.15).

For Bernard, this vision of love calls forth love: "The more surely you know yourself loved, the easier you will find it to love in return." He calls this the "wounds of love" (*On Loving God* III.7, 179), and these wounds inspire a conviction that we have loved too little: "God, then, loves, and loves with all his being, for the whole Trinity loves—if the word 'whole' can be used of the infinite, the incomprehensible, absolute Being" (IV.13, 184). And thus we ought to love "without measure" the one who loved us first (VI.16). We are hemmed in by love. It approaches from without, wells up within, unfolds in new ways within time: "I said before that God is the cause of loving God. I spoke the truth, for he is both the efficient and the final cause. He himself provides the occasion. He himself creates the longing. He himself fulfills the desire. He himself causes himself to be (or rather to be made) such that he should be loved" (VI.22, 178).

What Meister Eckhart did for Dionysius, the fourteenth-century English mystic and visionary Julian of Norwich (1342–ca. 1416) did for Bernard of Clairvaux. That is, both late medieval authors, writing in the vernacular (Eckhart in Middle High German and Julian in Middle English), came upon the teachings of masters of depth and genius (Dionysius as "master of darkness" and Bernard as the great teacher of the love of/for God) and by translating their thought into the linguistic register of the vernacular, new for theology, were able to let the power of their meditation rush forth—a power that had been dammed up, as it were, in the elegant rhetorical structures of the classical languages. In contrast to Bernard's famous, baroque eloquence, Julian's book, she claims, was made by a "simple, unlettered creature, living in this mortal flesh" (*Showings* II, 177).[8] In contrast to the fancy *letterae* of the classical languages, Julian wrote in what she and her contemporaries thought of as the language of hearth, home, cradle, and kin, as opposed to the language of law courts, medical schools, and lecture rooms. Julian's language was associated with nursing mothers and familiar conversations with kin. It was, in her words, "homely."

This is at least one of the secrets of the power of the *Showings*, a book containing sixteen visions given to Julian when she was on the verge of death at the age of thirty. This obscure fourteenth-century nun from northern England longed for what she called a "mind of the passion" (*Showings* II, 178) and thus over the whole of her life asked for only three things: "The first was recollection of the Passion. The second was bodily sickness. The third was to have, of God's gift, three wounds. As to the first, it seemed to me that I had some feeling for the Passion of Christ, but still I desired to have more by the grace of God. I thought that I wished that I had been at that time with Magdalen and with the others who were Christ's lovers, so that I might have seen with my own eyes the Passion which our Lord suffered for me, so that I might have suffered with him as others did who loved him" (II, 177–78).

Like many in her time, gentle Julian was obsessed with Christ's passion. A century and a half earlier, Thomas of Celano had written the poem "Stabat Mater," which imagines what it would have been like to stand at the foot of the cross, staring up at Christ and then turning to see his mother standing nearby. Similarly, the masterpieces of Rogier van der Weyden and Fra Angelico regularly picture John, Mary, and Mary Magdalene grieving at the foot of the cross, paradigms for our own prayerful, affective responses to Christ. Matthias Grünewald, in a sixteenth-century painting with a dark black background, created probably the most powerful image in Western art (Isenheim Altarpiece), with Christ covered in plague sores and Mary Magdalene, devastated and heartbroken, kneeling at the foot of the cross with hands grasped in dolorous prayer. And even Johann Sebastian Bach, centuries later, used his music to depict grief, including employing a flute to make a little trickling sound to mimic the tears of Mary Magdalene (listen to his "Buss und Reu" [Repentance and Regret] in *St. Matthew's Passion*). Artistic depictions of the passion like this saturated the world of Julian. We shouldn't be surprised, then, to learn that her visions were occasioned by her meditative gaze at a painted crucifix: "My curate [was sent for] to be present at my end. . . .

By that time my eyes were fixed, and I could not speak. [He] set the cross before my face and said: Daughter, I have brought you the image of your saviour. Look at it and take comfort from it" (*Showings* III, 180). Thus, like her devout contemporaries, Julian longed to be close to Christ, to retroactively comfort him in that moment in which he felt so alone and, in this way, to knit her heart together with his by absorbing his passion into her heart.

And all of this was granted to Julian. She was given the "gift" of sickness ("I wanted to have every kind of pain, bodily and spiritual, which I should have if I had died, every fear and temptation from devils, and every other kind of pain except the departure of the spirit. I intended this because I wanted to be purged by God's mercy, and afterwards live more to his glory because of that sickness," *Showings* II, 178). For three days and nights Julian lay in bed, so sick that all those around her expected her to die. It was then that she was given a series of visions while she meditated on the painted crucifix. She got to witness, as if firsthand, what Christ endured. She stared "with bodily vision into the face of the crucifix" and saw "contempt, foul spitting, buffeting, and many long-drawn pains, more than I can tell; and his colour often changed. At one time I saw how half his face, beginning at the ear, became covered with dried blood, until it was caked to the middle of his face, and then the other side was caked in the same fashion. . . . This I saw bodily, frighteningly and dimly" (X, 193). At other points Julian is made to witness and feel the breaking of "the tender flesh" (XII) or the drying of Christ's flesh (that is, his "thirst," XVI), a ghastly vision that is comparable to Grünewald's image of Christ writhing in pain.

Throughout her *Showings*, Julian's "homely" language and metaphors make these scenes all the more intense. It's so easy, when talking about spiritual things, to lose the freshness of the sense of compassion through abstract theological terms, but Julian's homely metaphors break through this. When she describes Christ's thirst, she uses the image of desiccated fruit ("This was a painful change to watch, this deep drying, and his nose shrivelled and dried up as I saw; and the sweet body turned brown and black, completely changed and transformed into a shrivelled image of death. For at the time when our blessed savior died upon the Cross, there was a dry, bitter wind," *Showings* XVI, 206). When she describes the Lord's bleeding from his crown of thorns, she likens "the copiousness" of his blood to "drops of water which fall from the eaves of a house after a great shower of rain, falling so thick that no human ingenuity can count them. And in their roundness as they spread over the forehead they were like a her-ring's scales" (VII, 188). In another place, Julian likens Christ's dried-out skin to a "dry board which has aged" (XVII, 208). And finally, Julian has a spiritual vision of the abundance and "effi-cacy" of the blood of Christ. She sees it flowing from the cross and, like a great redemptive tsunami, covering all the earth before seeping down through the ground and filling up all of hell (XII, 200). Julian's "homely" language is moving and impossible to ignore: it is the sound of breaking glass or hoarse screeching. In its ordinariness it is able to do what elaborate, fugue-like rhetoric cannot.

If this were all that Julian had done, we would have a remark-able vernacular masterpiece that—to return to the metaphor one last time—performs in us what Hugh of Balma, Bernard of Clair-vaux, and Guigo II talked about: the "experience" of God and the "wisdom of the spirit." But although Julian had only requested three gifts in order to help her gain "the mind of the passion," she got more than she requested. She did not just enter into affective union with the Lord through a "bodily vision" of the passion; she was also given a mysterious revelation of God's "kindness," in two senses: the ineffable goodness that moved God to make, sustain, and direct the world, as well as his strange insistence on dwelling with us and among us as one of us (his "kindred-ness"). And it is this vision of goodness that transforms even the gruesome instruments of the passion into—if it can be believed—happy and joyful expressions of goodness. In Julian, the world is all love, and every creature a revelation of divine kindness.

For this depiction of the shocking "kindness" of God, Julian resorts again to familiar images drawn from hearth and home: God is our "clothing" that "wraps and enfolds us for love, embraces us and shelters us, surrounds us for his love, which is so tender that he may never desert us." The world is like a hazelnut held in the palm of his hand: "I looked at it with the eye of my understanding and thought: What can this be? I was amazed that it could last, for I thought that because of its littleness it would suddenly have fallen into nothing. And I was answered in my understanding: It lasts and always will, because God loves it; and thus everything has being through the love of God" (*Showings* V, 183). Elsewhere, Julian makes the Augustinian point—in her own "homely" way—that God is nearer to me than I am to myself: "For as the body is clad in the cloth, and the flesh in the skin, and the bones in the flesh, and the heart in the trunk, so are we, soul and body, clad and enclosed in the goodness of God. Yes, and more closely" (XVI, 186). In other words, just as I have no control over my pulse and other biological functions but am still sustained by their operation, so too am I sustained, driven, and nourished by the goodness of God, as if the goodness of God is something I drink in at the cellular level. But Julian is at her best when describing God's "kindness" in the familiar sense. At one point she relates a vision of heaven, which appears to her to be a great medieval banquet; but the Lord, rather than being attended to by his servants, attends to each of them individually, thanking those who gave up their youth to his service: "And so that I might understand this, he showed me this plain example. It is the greatest honour which a majestic king or a great lord can do for a poor servant, to be familiar with him; and especially if he makes this known himself, privately and publicly, with great sincerity and happy mien" (VII, 188).

Julian's greatest feat in the *Showings* is to reread even the tragic failure of humanity (sin) in a major key. Indeed, Julian worries about this throughout the book. She feels the pain that Jesus suffered to be more severe than any and all pains endured by any human throughout time, and her heart breaks so much for Jesus's pain that, she says, she'd rather suffer with Jesus in hell than have heaven without him (*Showings* XX). When Jesus was suffering on the cross, all of nature wobbled and came dangerously close to evaporating from existence (XIX). Given how in tune Julian is with the suffering of the Lord, she is astonished to find that God is not angry about having to endure such intense and humiliating pain on humanity's behalf: "For I know by the ordinary teaching of Holy Church and by my own feeling that the blame of our sins continually hangs upon us, from the first man until the time that we come up into heaven. This, then, was my astonishment, that I saw our Lord God showing no more blame to us than if we were as pure and as holy as the angels are in heaven" (XL, 266). Then, in the famous chapter 51, Julian has another vision meant to explain this. She sees a servant who loves his Lord standing in attendance, waiting to rush forth eagerly to fulfill whatever is asked of him. The Lord, who reciprocates his servant's love, gives him an order, and he dashes off to obey it, but he stumbles, falls into a pit, and hurts himself badly. In the meantime, the Lord feels nothing but sorrow for his mishap. This, Julian tells us, is the astonishing message given to her by means of this vision. At no point does God angrily scold or turn his face from us. He merely laments that, given our injuries, we have become momentarily incapable of reciprocating his love. How can this be? At one and the same moment, the servant who dashes off is both Adam (and thus all of humanity) and Christ (and thus all of humanity re-deemed). Although human beings stumbled and fell into the ditch, God "instantly," as it were, compensated for it. We cannot "trick" God into revealing a face of wrath toward humanity! For Julian, however badly we stumble, God has already compensated for it in advance. God is the face of mercy in every moment in time.

It is true, then, that Julian's raw, image-filled descriptions of her "showings" are stirring, but her main achievement is to reread all those images of pain and sorrow as revelations of love. Beneath the surface, all is love, in woe or in well. In fact, even a brutal event such as Christ's passion met with the Trinity's approval. God's craftsmanship did not end with the construction of the world; rather, no matter what we might foist upon it or how we might twist, smear, or stain it, God has an inventive, loving strategy to make it all clean again.

John Ruusbroec: The Maelstrom of God's Glory

The extraordinary John Ruusbroec (1293–1381), who lived in fourteenth-century Brabant (modern northeastern Belgium and southwestern Netherlands), combined almost all of the individual elements we have isolated and discussed throughout this book: he read the "Blessed Dionysius," but he also wrote in the vernacular (medieval Dutch) and emphasized the affective elements of spirituality. Within his works, then, we find simultaneously that sense of God's "rushing out" in love and the "drawing in" toward the heart of the abyss.

For example, in his short *The Sparkling Stone*, Ruusbroec outlines how the soul may ascend to God. You must begin by following the moral precepts of Christianity, before moving on to develop a sense of fervent interiority, ascending still higher to a stage of contemplation, and coming to a stage of "flowing out"—that is, a stage in which mystical contemplation and public charity are fully combined in what he calls "the common life" (because it mingles the contemplative and active virtues).[9] As usual, we find that one gets to these highest levels of mystical contemplation only by passing through the lower stages of morality (à la Hugh of Balma) and then spiritual exercises of fervency ("Such exercises are thanksgiving, praise, worship, devout prayers, fervent affection," *Sparkling Stone*, 157). If you're an immoral person, or even just dangerously passionate, then yoga or "finding God in nature" does no good. You must have a heart "unencumbered by images" and come to possess a "spiritual freedom" in terms of desire: "If a person is to become spiritual he must renounce all fleshly affection and cleave to God alone" (157).

But as we have seen throughout this book, "being good" is not the goal. We must pass beyond the lower stages of morality and rise to a level of spiritual fervor in which we long for nothing besides the glory of God to be loved: "By means of these interior exercises a person attains the third thing necessary for a spiritual life [that is, after becoming "free from images" and achieving "spiritual freedom"], which is that he experiences spiritual union with God. Whoever, then, in his interior exercises ascends freely and without images to his God and intends nothing but God's glory will savor God's goodness and will experience true interior union with God" (*Sparkling Stone*, 157).

As extraordinary as this deeply connected state of affective union with God is, it is only preparation for an even deeper spiritual condition. To describe it, Ruusbroec, like an organist on an old-world instrument in an ancient chapel, has to pull out all the stops, use all the pedals and keyboards, and combine rhetoric and metaphors into a kind of fugue, because in the contemplative state one experiences "the depth of his being as having no ground": "The union with God which a spiritual person experiences . . . is one which is without ground, that is, it is infinitely deep, infinitely high, and infinitely long and wide. In this very manifestation a person's spirit realizes that, by means of love, it has itself been immersed in this depth, raised to this height, and sent forth into this length" (*Sparkling Stone*, 158). The contemplative "renounces himself" and comes to "the inmost part of his spirit in a state of bareness and freedom," where "an eternal light is revealed to him, and in this light he experiences the eternal call of God's Unity. He also feels himself to be an eternal fire of love, which desires above all else to be one with God" (158). In Ruusbroec's description, you feel that you are falling into a bottomless chasm, seeing a shining light, being scorched by a flame, and wandering in a desert of absolute stillness all at once. This is the "eternal call of God's Unity" that "creates in the spirit an eternal fire of love," but "no one can experience or possess this simple Unity of God unless he stands before God in measureless resplendence and in love that is above reason and devoid of a particular form. . . . The spirit remains constantly on fire within itself, for its love is eternal; it also feels that it is constantly being consumed in the fire of love" (159).

I don't think there's any other passage quite like the one I am about to quote—in which a medieval author creates such a sublimely moving image of God's love—except perhaps in Dante. Every single metaphor I have carefully pulled out and separated throughout this book collides in a kind of spiritual hurricane of intense devotion. Loving God is falling, soaring, being immersed, melted down, suddenly flying, building your home over an abyss. It is fire, gravity, light, depth, height, and motion. Here's how Ruusbroec puts it:

> You can thus see that this Unity of God which draws all things to itself is nothing other than a love which has no ground and which lovingly draws the Father and the Son and all that lives in them into a state of eternal enjoyment. In this love we will ceaselessly burn and be consumed by fire for all eternity, for in this lies the blessedness of all spirits. For this reason we must place our entire life on the foundation of a groundless abyss. Then we will be able to plunge eternally in love and immerse ourselves in a depth which has no ground. Through the same love we will ascend and transcend ourselves as we rise to an incomprehensible height. In this formless love we will wander about, and it will lead us to the measureless breadth of God's love. In it we will flow forth and flow out of ourselves into the uncomprehended abundance of God's riches and goodness. In it we will also melt and be dissolved, revolve and be eternally whirled round in the maelstrom of God's glory. (*Sparkling Stone*, 158–59)

What is extraordinary, though, is that this experience is, as it were, always around us (as we've seen Eckhart describe it). Love, like a kind of vast "field" (like gravity or electromagnetism), is always around us, pulling and tugging, but we only become aware of it—and let it operate within us—when we become like it (a combination of Augustine and Eckhart): "The more he perceives this attraction and call, the more he feels it, the more he desires to be one with God" (*Sparkling Stone*, 158–59). It's as if we dwell at the bottom of an ocean of love that we have ceased to notice because it is ubiquitous, but it exerts pressure on us, waiting for the least excuse of an invitation to rush in: "As long as a sinner wishes to remain in the service of sin, he remains deaf and blind and is incapable of tasting or feeling all the good things which God desires to work in him" (163).

Ruusbroec also recycles from Eckhart the idea of the bare spiritual desert, as well as the "nudity" of the soul, describing mysticism as being "raised up through love to the open bareness of our mind" (*Sparkling Stone*, 171), where "bare love can envelop us" (170), "when we go out of ourselves into a dark, modeless state which has no ground," where we can "neither speak about nor remain silent about it" (171), where we "are swallowed up above reason and apart from reason in the deep stillness of the Godhead" (172). Ruusbroec also refers to this as "being scorched" (181), being immersed (176), "falling asleep in God" (183), and "falling into the groundless abyss of our eternal blessedness" (176), as well as walking through a desert in which we encounter the "imageless bareness which is God himself" (158). The mind is raised far beyond the level of virtue, to the place where with "the simple gaze" we stare "with open mind into the divine resplendence" (167). The experience is so intense that we grow afraid and hesitant before making the plunge: we "retain something of [our] own [selves] and so are not consumed and burnt to nought in the unity of love. Even though [we] wish to live constantly in God's service and please him forever, [we] do not wish to die in God to all the self-centeredness of [our] spirit" (167).

As I have said, few medieval authors managed to capture the primal, visceral, physiological feeling of falling or soaring quite like Ruusbroec. Maybe only Dante. And Ruusbroec's genius is in how he gives us a God who is neither sentimental and saccharine nor remote and aloof, but transcendent in his goodness. This is a God you can long for.

Nicholas of Cusa

Nicholas of Cusa (also known as Cusanus; 1401–1464) was a fifteenth-century German cardinal who lived on the boundary of the medieval and modern worlds. A little over a century after his death, modern mathematics, a heliocentric universe, and empirical approaches to the natural world were commonplace, but hints of all those developments may be found already in Cusanus as applied theology. For this reason he has received a lot of attention lately for how his prescient use of mathematics anticipates calculus and set theory; for his interest in contemporary painting, including visual tricks; and for his fascinating "empirical" approach to thought experiments, which anticipates the idea of producing *experientia* in Robert Boyle and Isaac Newton.[10] He shares company with only a few other philosophers and theologians who possessed a deeply medieval sense for the iconicity of the visible cosmos but were also interested in using the new "languages" of modernity (mathematics and empirical science). What interests me, though, is what I want to call Nicholas's "spiritual calculus" (which later influenced Leibniz's discovery of calculus)—that is, his use of thought experiments that stretch their content to their limits as a way of visualizing the dynamic spiritual realities that underlie them.

For example, in his brief treatise *On Seeking God*, Nicholas addresses a spiritual brother who is eager to seek God but doesn't know where to begin.[11] We can sympathize with him. So many of these ancient treatises talk about God and unity and goodness, but when it comes to the question, "What do I actually do to get at what you're describing?" we're sometimes lost. Right away, Cusanus, in language that echoes Plotinus and Augustine, tells him that the path to God is a paradoxical ascent accomplished by a descent within. The interior turn: we're on familiar ground. But then Cusanus provides a series of meditations—small metaphysical thought experiments—to help accomplish this in his brother's mind: "It is my intent that the meditation of us both may thereby be stirred, and that by an intellectual ascent the inner person may be more and more transformed from light to light until in clear recognition and through the light of glory one enters into the joy of one's Lord" (*On Seeking God* 16, 217). This is where things get interesting.

Nicholas proposes first to interrogate the spiritual significance of sight. He imagines the region of visible things and how all things within the world present themselves in different colors. Sight, though, does not "belong" to the region of the visible but is, rather, situated above all things of color. Sight does not possess color because, in order to be sight, it must be able to see every color. In this way, sight is a kind of potentiality of all possible colors. Cusanus concludes, "When we regard the world of visible things with our intellect and ask whether a knowledge of sight is found in it, all this world of color will be ignorant of sight, since it perceives nothing that is not colored" (*On Seeking God* 22, 218–19). In other words, in this fascinating thought experiment, the mere property of having color (of "being blue" or "being red") does not accompany a perception of blueness or redness. The ability to perceive color is different from being color.

But Nicholas pursues the question further. He imagines asking the colors, "In your opinion, what 'color' is sight?" The colors are confused. They can only think in terms of "being color," and so the best they can do is suggest that perhaps white is the closest thing to sight because it is most like all the colors at once. But clearly, any proposed answer would fail to get at what sight is, and, in fact, the colors, could we talk to them, would have a hard time trusting us when we say that there is such a thing as sight. "Indeed, it cannot attain that sight is anything at all, since apart from color the visible world does not attain anything but judges that everything not colored is not something." And thus the world of color casts about within its limited vocabulary, frustrated that every meaningful term fails: "Among all the names that can be named . . . none befits sight, indeed, neither the name 'white' nor 'black,' nor that of the whole mixture of colors, since neither the name of 'white' and 'non-white' together nor that of 'black' and 'non-black' together befit sight" (*On Seeking God* 22, 219). Sight is, so to speak, on a third dimensional axis at a right angle to the two-dimensional world of colors. No combination of them will adequately "befit" the pure potentiality of color in sight.

How does Nicholas apply this thought experiment to God and mystical theology? Our rationality can take up all possible modes of argumentation: some reasons are necessary, others possible, some contingent, some impossible (*On Seeking God* 25). But all of those arguments are contained within our minds, just as colors unfold within sight. Nicholas goes one more step. If you consider all the intellects as analogous to the fields of colors, is there some "sight" in which they all participate? That is, if we start to "think away" all that is limiting by means of being particular, we are left with a pure light of understanding. This is the thought experiment that helps us approach God, who has no body and thus no quantity, place, form, or position. We have to reject even reason and intellect as too limiting for that which embraces everything in simultaneity: "When, therefore, you conceive that God is better than can be conceived, you reject everything that is limited and contracted. . . . But if you seek further, you find nothing in yourself like God, but rather you affirm that God is above all these as the cause, beginning, and light of life of your intellective soul" (*On Seeking God* 49, 231). By plunging within, we have come to the apex of reality. We're back to Augustine.

But for Nicholas's endlessly curious mind, there are so many of these ascending paths all around me—that is, so many starting points for this kind of ascent throughout nature! For this reason, as Cusanus reflects at the beginning of the treatise, we *will* find God if we look for him, because "Paul says, God is not far from anyone, for in God we exist, live, and move. . . . Each time I read the Acts of the Apostles I marvel at this process of thought" (*On Seeking God* 17–18, 217). Indeed, for Nicholas, God is greedy to be known: "For God who is everywhere is impossible not to find if God is sought in the right way" (31, 223). Later he adds that God is the God of self-disclosure: "And God wills to be sought and wills to give to seekers the light without which they are unable to seek God. God wills to be sought, and God also wills to be apprehended, for it is God's will to uncover and to disclose Godself to those who seek" (39, 226). It's as if God discloses himself in as many ways as possible.

For example, at another point Nicholas expresses admiration for even the humble mustard seed, which can "stir us in wonder at our God" (*On Seeking God* 44, 228). Within the tiny seed is the life that will grow into a tree, but then the tree, when fully grown, will drop other seeds that will become trees that will drop more seeds, such that "if its potential should be unfolded in actuality, this sensible world would not suffice, nor indeed, would ten or a thousand or all the worlds that one could count" (44, 228). But Nicholas goes on to marvel that what is even more miraculous is that my mind can perform this kind of spiritual calculus—that I can intellectively surpass "all capacity of the whole sensible world, and not only of this one world but also of an infinite number of worlds. . . . How great a magnitude there is in our intellect! . . . Through similar ascents, you will be able to ascend from the power of the millet seed and likewise from the power of all vegetable and animal seeds. The power of no seed is less than that of the mustard seed, and there are an infinite number of such seeds. Oh how great is our God, who is the actuality of all potency!" (45, 228–29). That last part is important, because even if all the potentialities in every seed were unfolded into their infinities, the world would still be but a shadowy explication of God, just as the world of colors would be a shadowy imitation of sight.

In this way, Nicholas delights in the many ways of ascent. He sees the world as full of places in which infinity is hidden away.

In his most famous work, *On Learned Ignorance*, he reflects on how creatures are images "of that single, infinite Form, as if the creature were an occasioned god. . . . The infinite form is received only in a finite way; consequently, every creature is, as it were, a finite infinity or a created god" (*On Learned Ignorance* 104, 134). The universe, then, is a kind of infinity of micro-infinities, a set of creatures each of which constitutes a unity emerging out of the pure potentiality of matter. Thus, when Nicholas surveys the world in his mind's eye, he sees it as a great pasture in which the mind can play, frolic, and gambol.

> If you tread upon [a certain path], it will be your own path and . . . on it you will take delight because of its beauty and the abundance of fruit found all around it. Apply yourself, therefore, by increased acts and contemplative ascents, and you will find pastures that augment and strengthen you on your journey and daily inflame you more in desire. For our intellectual spirit has the power of fire within it. It has been sent by God to earth for no other end than to glow and to spring up in flame. It increases when it is excited by wonder, as if wind blowing on fire excites its potency to actuality. Therefore, through the knowledge of the works of God we marvel at eternal wisdom and are stirred by an external wind of works and of creatures of such various powers and operations that our desire may burst into love of the Creator and into a contemplation of that wisdom that has wonderfully ordered all things. (*On Seeking God* 43, 228)

For Nicholas the world is almost too full, almost painfully joyful. There's too much goodness to take in, too much variety. God is too good, too benign, too loving toward us. He didn't choose just one path to make himself known but an infinite number of them, and they're all enveloping us, clamoring for our attention.

This, then, I think, is what we have lost in modernity: a sense of the world as supersaturated by an infinite number of joys pressing in on us, surrounding us, rushing toward us. For the premodern world, visible nature can give us a glimpse of an infinitely benign God. In this way, both Cusanus and John Ruusbroec help us recover a vision of what I have called the wildness of the spiritual life—indeed, the wildness of God. And it is this vision that has, all of a sudden, come to appear so urgent again.

Notes

Introduction

1. Meister Eckhart, Sermon 3, in *Meister Eckhart: Selected Writings*, trans. Oliver Davies, Penguin Classics (London: Penguin, 1994), 121–22. This sermon is Sermon 17 in *Meister Eckhart: Sermons and Treatises*, trans. M. O'C. Walshe (London: Element, 1987), 141–45. Walshe's is an older, statelier, and more archaic translation, but it is the most convenient of all modern translations, given that it is a collected work. Unless noted otherwise, all quotations of Eckhart in this introduction come from Walshe's translation.

2. See the prelude in George Eliot, *Middlemarch* (New York: Caldwell, n.d.), Project Gutenberg, https://www.gutenberg.org/files/145/145-h/145-h.htm#pref01:

> Who that cares much to know the history of man, and how the mysterious mixture behaves under the varying experiments of Time, has not dwelt, at least briefly, on the life of Saint Theresa, has not smiled with some gentleness at the thought of the little girl walking forth one morning hand-in-hand with her still smaller brother, to go and seek martyrdom in the country of the Moors? Out they toddled from rugged Avila, wide-eyed and helpless-looking as two fawns, but with human hearts, already beating to a national idea; until domestic reality met them in the shape of uncles, and turned them back from their great resolve. That child-pilgrimage was a fit beginning. Theresa's passionate, ideal nature demanded an epic life: what were many-volumed romances of chivalry and the social conquests of a brilliant girl to her? Her flame quickly burned up that light fuel; and, fed from within, soared after some illimitable satisfaction, some object which would never justify weariness, which would reconcile self-despair with the rapturous consciousness of life beyond self. She found her epos in the reform of a religious order.

3. B. B. Warfield, *The Works of Benjamin B. Warfield* (Grand Rapids: Baker, 1991), 9:653. And see William Mueller's March 30, 1962, article in *Christianity*

Today ("The Mystical Union") for another good example of Protestant anxiety about the term "mysticism."

4. C. S. Lewis, *The Weight of Glory and Other Addresses* (New York: Touchstone, 1996), 38.

5. Pope Emeritus Benedict XVI addressed the relationship between such Greek thinking and faith in his (in)famous Regensburg address.

6. See Bernard McGinn, *The Mystical Thought of Meister Eckhart: The Man from Whom God Hid Nothing* (New York: Crossroad, 2001), 183n2.

7. Lewis, *Weight of Glory*, 39.

8. This phenomenon existed in antiquity too! See Bernard McGinn, *The Foundations of Mysticism: Origins to the Fifth Century* (New York: Crossroad, 1991), 142.

9. I'm thinking of a wonderful paper on Nicholas of Cusa and infinite desire I heard David Bentley Hart read at the University of Notre Dame in fall 2019. Hart, "Cusanus on Beauty and the Infinite," Cusanus Today conference, University of Notre Dame, September 20, 2019.

10. In fact, presence is the key component of mysticism, according to Bernard McGinn, the leading expert on mysticism of our day: "We can say that the mystical element in Christianity is that part of its belief and practices that concerns the preparation for, the consciousness of, and the reaction to what can be described as the immediate or direct presence of God" (*Foundations of Mysticism*, xvii).

11. Bernard McGinn, "The Abyss of Love," in *The Joy of Learning and the Love of God*, ed. Rozanne Elder (Kalamazoo, MI: Cistercian Publications), 95–120.

12. Andrew Louth describes this as the "ability to let go and pass beyond, an activity learnt by exercise at lower levels: this is the fruit of intellectual purification. Trouillard calls this *générosité intellectuelle*, a rarer gift than moral generosity" (*The Origins of the Christian Mystical Tradition: From Plato to Denys* [Oxford: Clarendon, 1981], 45).

13. "For the Christian [the deeper self] is the point where God and soul touch. . . . It is what Tauler called 'the ground of the soul' and Eckhart 'the little castle.' Catherine of Siena speaks of the 'interior home of the heart,' Teresa of the 'inner castle,' and John of the Cross of the 'house at rest . . . in darkness and concealment.' All these metaphors suggest a secret dwelling where God resides" (Louis Dupré, *The Deeper Life: An Introduction to Christian Mysticism* [New York: Crossroad, 1981], 24).

14. For translations of the *Confessions*, I use *Augustine: Confessions*, trans. F. J. Sheed (Indianapolis: Hackett, 2006). Parenthetical citations include the book and section numbers from the *Confessions* and the page number from this edition.

15. Charles Taylor, *A Secular Age* (Cambridge, MA: Belknap, 2007), 553.

16. Louis Dupré uses these terms in reference to "an entire age that has lost the direct presence of the sacred and that has replaced transcendence by self-transcending. We may call the prevailing climate a-theistic, not because faith has disappeared in our time, but because the question whether we believe in God or not, retains little or no practical bearing upon our lives" (*Deeper Life*,

14). For a great introduction to Dupré, see Peter Casarella's excellent "'Modern Forms with Traditional Spiritual Content': On Louis Dupré's Contribution to Christian Theology," in *Christian Spirituality and the Culture of Modernity: The Thought of Louis Dupré*, ed. Peter J. Casarella and George P. Schner (Grand Rapids: Eerdmans, 1998), 275–310.

17. Taylor, *Secular Age*, 25.

18. For what it felt like to live in an "enchanted cosmos," see my "Why Read Old Books? Recovering the Buried Past," in *Falling Inward: Humanities in the Age of Technology* (Providence: Cluny Press, 2018), 41–68; see also Charles Taylor, "The Bulwarks of Belief," in *A Secular Age*, 25–89.

19. For such premodern visions of the cosmos, see C. S. Lewis, *The Discarded Image* (Cambridge: Cambridge University Press, 2012). My forthcoming book will also treat this: *The Medieval Mind of C. S. Lewis* (Downers Grove, IL: InterVarsity).

20. See Steve Shapin's excellent "What Was the Knowledge For?," in *The Scientific Revolution* (Chicago: University of Chicago Press, 1996), 119–66; Eugene Klaaren, *Religious Origins of Modern Science: Belief in Creation in Seventeenth-Century Thought* (Grand Rapids: Eerdmans, 1977); and John Henry, "Religion and the Scientific Revolution," in *The Cambridge Companion to Science and Religion*, ed. Peter Harrison (Cambridge: Cambridge University Press, 2010), 39–58.

21. Taylor, *Secular Age*, 540.

22. Taylor, *Secular Age*, 554.

23. Louis Dupré, "The Religious Crisis of Our Culture," *Yale Review* 65 (1976): 213.

24. Dupré, "Religious Crisis of Our Culture," 214.

25. Murray Roston, *Changing Perspectives in Literature and the Visual Arts, 1650–1820* (Princeton: Princeton University Press, 1990), 197–98.

26. Christian Smith and Melinda Lundquist Denton, *Soul Searching: The Religious and Spiritual Lives of American Teenagers* (Oxford: Oxford University Press, 2005), 165–66.

27. Kenda Creasy Dean, *Almost Christian: What the Faith of Our Teenagers Is Telling the American Church* (Oxford: Oxford University Press, 2010), 25–44.

28. Ulrich Lehner, *God Is Not Nice: Rejecting Pop Culture Theology and Discovering the God Worth Living For* (South Bend, IN: Ave Maria, 2017), 2.

29. Lehner, *God Is Not Nice*, ix, citing Niebuhr, *Kingdom of God in America* (1937; repr., Middletown, CT: Wesleyan University Press, 1988), 193. Compare Karl Rahner's assessment: "We live in an age in which the question is not so much how as sinners we may gain access to a gracious God who will justify us; on the contrary the impression is that it is God—if there is a God—who must justify himself to his creatures in their distress, while they for their part have no need of justification" ("The Christian Living Formerly and Today," in *Theological Investigations*, trans. David Bourke [New York: Seabury, 1971], 7:12).

30. The standard introduction to mysticism is Bernard McGinn's series The Presence of God: A History of Western Christian Mysticism. His life's work has been dedicated to tracing the history of Christian mysticism; at the time of

writing the series comprises six volumes (some of them having multiple parts): 1. *The Foundations of Mysticism* (cited above); 2. *The Growth of Mysticism* (from Gregory the Great to the "Twelfth-Century Reformation," including the Cistercian movement and the Abbey of St. Victor); 3. *The Flowering of Mysticism* (on the new mendicant piety, especially that of the Franciscans); 4. *The Harvest of Mysticism in Medieval Germany* (on Meister Eckhart and his followers); 5. *The Varieties of Vernacular Mysticism* (1350–1550); 6a. *Mysticism in the Reformation*; 6b. *Mysticism in the Golden Age of Spain*; 6c. *The Persistence of Mysticism in Catholic Europe.*

In addition to McGinn's work, I admire Andrew Louth's much shorter but beautifully moving *The Origins of the Christian Mystical Tradition* (cited above). See also *The Oxford Handbook of Mystical Theology*, ed. Edward Howells and Mark A. McIntosh (Oxford: Oxford University Press, 2020); and *The Cambridge Companion to Christian Mysticism*, ed. Amy Hollywood and Patricia Z. Beckman (New York: Cambridge University Press, 2012), which are both organized by themes as opposed to historical development.

With that said, if this volume were to double its length and thereby cease to be an introduction, the ten authors I would most need to include are (in no particular order) (1) Symeon the New Theologian, (2) Catherine of Siena, (3) Hildegard of Bingen, (4) Julian of Norwich, (5) Isaac of Stella, (6a) Johannes Tauler, (6b) Henry Suso, (7) Thomas Aquinas, (8) Richard of St. Victor, (9) Origen, and (10) Clement of Alexandria.

31. Hildegard of Bingen, *Scivias* 1.1, in *Hildegard of Bingen: Scivias*, trans. Columba Hart and Jane Bishop, Classics of Western Spirituality (Mahwah, NJ: Paulist Press, 1990), 67–68.

32. Hildegard of Bingen, *Scivias* 3.13 (533).

33. Hildegard of Bingen, *Scivias* 1.prologue (60).

34. Hildegard of Bingen, *Scivias* 1.prologue (59–60).

35. Hildegard of Bingen, *Scivias* 2.1 (149).

36. Hildegard of Bingen, *Scivias* 1.prologue (60).

37. Gregory the Great, *Moral Reflections on the Book of Job* 5.30.53, vol. 1, trans. Brian Kerns (Collegeville, MN: Liturgical Press, 2014), 352.

Chapter 1: The Christian of the Future in the Desert of Modernity

1. For a view of the world as "closed," just walk into a bookstore and pull a book off the shelf in the science section! Carl Sagan and the New Atheists are good examples of what Taylor is talking about. For a recent depiction of the "closed" view, see Steven Pinker, *Enlightenment Now: The Case for Reason, Science, Humanism, and Progress* (New York: Viking, 2018). See also, for example, physicist Steven Weinberg, who

> claims that as the universe has grown more comprehensible to science "the more pointless it also seems." Pondering Weinberg's sentiments, astronomer Margaret Geller essentially agrees: "Does [the universe] have a point? I don't know. It's not clear that it matters. I guess it's a kind of statement that I would never make. . . . It's just a physical system, what point is there?" Also

responding to Weinberg, physicist Marc Davis reflects: "I try not to think about the question [of cosmic purpose] too much, because all too often I agree with Steven Weinberg, and it's rather depressing." (John Haught, "Science, God, and Cosmic Purpose," in *The Cambridge Companion to Science and Religion*, ed. Peter Harrison [Cambridge: Cambridge University Press, 2010], 263) For the alternative, "open" view—that the "infinity" of the world is a figuring forth of the mind of God—see Ernest Tuveson, "Space, Deity, and the 'Natural Sublime,'" *Modern Language Quarterly* 12 (1951): 20–38. And see my "Nine Billion Names of God," to be published in *Church Life Journal*.

2. Louis Dupré, "The Religious Crisis of Our Culture," *Yale Review* 65 (1976): 215.

3. *The Essential René Guénon: Metaphysics, Tradition, and the Crisis of Modernity*, ed. John Herlihy (Bloomington, IN: World Wisdom, 2009), 3. Guénon is a prominent figure in Michel Houellebecq's meditation on the collapse of European culture in his novel *Submission* (trans. Lorin Stein [New York: Farrar, Straus & Giroux, 2015]).

4. Michael Rea, *The Hiddenness of God* (Oxford: Oxford University Press, 2018).

5. O'Connor was writing on September 6, 1955, to Betty Hester. See *The Habit of Being: Letters of Flannery O'Connor*, ed. Sally Fitzgerald (New York: Farrar, Straus & Giroux, 1979), 100. Similarly, Polish philosopher Leszek Kołakowski states, "Our age is marked by disquiet and uncertainty about God's presence or absence. The faithful worry about God, but their worries are really disguised worries about the world. Unbelievers worry about the world, but their worries are really disguised worries about God. . . . But for both the world abandoned by God is clearly a source of unease" (*Is God Happy? Selected Essays* [New York: Basic Books, 2006], 194–95).

6. See John Henry Newman, *An Essay in Aid of a Grammar of Assent* (Garden City, NY: Image Books, 1955), 309; and Newman, "Waiting for Christ," in *Parochial and Plain Sermons*, quoted in Dupré, "Spiritual Life in a Secular Age," *Daedalus* 111 (Winter 1982): 26.

7. Shūsaku Endō, *Silence*, trans. William Johnston (New York: Picador Classics, 2016), 57.

8. Endō, *Silence*, 62, 64.

9. "This was the sea that relentlessly washed the dead bodies of Mokichi and Ichizo, the sea that swallowed them up, the sea that, after their death, stretched out endlessly with unchanging expressions. And like the sea God was silent. His silence continued. . . . And the missionaries who spent three years crossing the sea to arrive at this country—what an illusion was theirs. Myself, too, wandering here over the desolate mountains—what an absurd situation! . . . I knew well, of course, that the greatest sin against God was despair; but the silence of God was something I could not fathom" (Endō, *Silence*, 72).

10. Endō, *Silence*, 67.

11. "He could no longer reckon how many days had passed since Easter or what saint's feast was celebrated today" (Endō, *Silence*, 91).

12. Endō, *Silence*, 98.

13. Endō, *Silence*, 179.

14. Rudolf Otto, *The Idea of the Holy*, trans. John Harvey (Oxford: Oxford University Press, 1958), 6. Subsequent page numbers from this work are in parentheses.

15. Mircea Eliade, *The Sacred and the Profane* (New York: Harcourt, 1987), 20.

16. Eliade, *The Sacred and the Profane*, 26.

17. Eliade, *The Sacred and the Profane*, 11–12.

18. Eliade, *The Sacred and the Profane*, 50, 64.

19. As Hans-Georg Gadamer put it in his 1980 speech "Praise of Theory," "Today, it seems, there is no need to assert that the future path of humanity depends on things other than technological inventiveness and skill in dealing with the bottlenecks of global industrialization" (*Praise of Theory: Speeches and Essays*, trans. Chris Dawson [New Haven: Yale University Press, 1998], 28). See also Edmund Husserl's famous 1935 Vienna Address, "Philosophy and the Crisis of European Man," in *Phenomenology and the Crisis of Philosophy*, trans. Quentin Lauer (New York: Harper Torchbooks, 1965), 149–92. And for a "history" of the future of this problem (the quest for domination at the price of meaning), see the Jewish philosopher Yuval Harari's *Homo Deus: A Brief History of Tomorrow* (New York: Harper Perennial, 2018). Harari's book explores a theme similar to that treated in C. S. Lewis's 1943 classic *The Abolition of Man*.

20. See Bernard McGinn, "The Future of Past Spiritual Traditions," *Spiritus: A Journal of Christian Spirituality* 15 (2015): 1–18.

21. Dupré, "Spiritual Life in a Secular Age," 21.

22. For this reason David Bentley Hart says that Christians should be grateful to the New Atheists because they've given us the motivation to return to the deep tradition and purify our picture of God (*The Experience of God: Being, Consciousness, Bliss* [New Haven: Yale University Press, 2014]). See also Denys Turner's inaugural lecture at Cambridge, "How to Be an Atheist," *New Blackfriars* 83 (July/August 2002): 317–35.

23. Michel de Certeau, *The Mystic Fable*, trans. Michael Smith, 2 vols. (Chicago: University of Chicago Press, 1992), 2:14.

24. See his 1954 Cambridge address, "De Descriptione Temporum," which is about the "dividing line" of historical ages.

25. Dupré, "Religious Crisis of Our Culture," 208.

26. Thomas Merton, "Mysticism in the Nuclear Age," in *A Thomas Merton Reader*, ed. Thomas McDonnell (New York: Image Books, 1974), 372. Subsequent page numbers from this work are in parentheses.

27. See Max Picard, *The World of Silence* (repr., Wichita: Eighth Day Press, 2002).

28. Thomas Merton, "Silence," in McDonnell, *Thomas Merton Reader*, 457.

29. Merton, "Silence," 459.

30. Merton, "Silence," 457.

31. Merton, "Silence," 458.

32. "The silence of the tongue and of the imagination dissolves the barrier between ourselves and the peace of things that exist only for God and not for themselves. But the silence of all inordinate desire dissolves the barrier between ourselves and God. Then we come to live in Him alone. Then mute beings no longer speak to us merely with their own silence. It is the Lord Who speaks to us, with a far deeper silence, hidden in the midst of our own selves" (Merton, "Silence," 458).

33. Karl Rahner, "The Christian Living Formerly and Today," in *Theological Investigations*, trans. David Bourke (New York: Seabury, 1971), 7:12.

34. Dupré, "Religious Crisis of Our Culture," 203. Charles Taylor makes the same point in "A Place for Transcendence?," in *Transcendence: Philosophy, Literature, and Theology Approach the Beyond*, ed. Regina Schwartz (New York: Routledge, 2004), 1–11.

35. Rahner, "Christian Living Formerly and Today," 14.

36. Dupré, "Religious Crisis of Our Culture," 213.

37. Dupré, "Religious Crisis of Our Culture," 210.

38. Dupré, "Spiritual Life in a Secular Age," in *Ignatian Spirituality in a Secular Age*, ed. George Schner (Waterloo, Ontario: Wilfrid Laurier University Press, 2006), 16.

39. Rahner, "Christian Living Formerly and Today," 13.

40. Rahner, "Christian Living Formerly and Today," 14.

41. Dupré, "Spiritual Life in a Secular Age," 19.

42. Dupré, "Spiritual Life in a Secular Age," 17.

43. Rahner, "Christian Living Formerly and Today," 15.

Chapter 2: Pagans Grope toward God

1. All quotations from Plato are from *Plato: Complete Works*, ed. John Cooper (Indianapolis: Hackett, 1997). Rather than page numbers, I use Stephanus numbers (the marginal numbers found in any edition).

2. "I have a divine or spiritual sign which Meletus has ridiculed in his deposition. This began when I was a child. It is a voice, and whenever it speaks it turns me away from something I am about to do, but it never encourages me to do anything" (Plato, *Apology* 29d).

3. There are many good translations of Plotinus's treatises (called the *Enneads*), but I use *Enneads*, trans. A. H. Armstrong, 6 vols., Loeb Classical Library (Cambridge, MA: Harvard University Press, 1969). The Roman numeral refers to the book number, and the Arabic numerals refer to the treatise and section numbers.

4. "It is barely possible for knowledge to be engendered . . . in a man naturally good; but if his nature is defective, as is that of most men . . . then not even Lynceus [famous for his eyesight] could make such a man see" ("Seventh Letter," 343e–344a).

5. For this characterization of the moral and intellectual aspects of the Greek philosophical life, I am indebted to my friends Lionel Yaceczko and Patrick Callahan, as well as to Pierre Hadot's *Philosophy as a Way of Life*, trans. Arnold

Davidson (London: Wiley-Blackwell, 1995), as well as Hadot's masterful *The Veil of Isis: An Essay on the History of the Idea of Nature*, trans. Michael Chase (Cambridge, MA: Belknap, 2008); Hadot, *Plotinus, or The Simplicity of Vision*, trans. Michael Chase (Chicago: University of Chicago Press, 1993); Thomas Szlezák, *Reading Plato*, trans. Graham Zanker (London: Routledge, 1999). See also John Dillon, "The Platonic Philosopher at Prayer," in *Platonic Theories of Prayer*, ed. John Dillon and Andrei Timotin (Leiden: Brill, 2016), 7–25; and Giovanni Reale, *A History of Ancient Philosophy*, ed. and trans. John R. Catan, 4 vols. (Albany, NY: SUNY Press, 1985–90). And see the moving lecture of John Rist, "The Perennial Importance of Plato," given April 2013 for the Faith and Reason initiative at the Franciscan University of Steubenville (available, at the time of writing, on YouTube at https://youtu.be/IMkahvgTCEE).

6. See John Dillon's discussion in "Platonic Philosopher at Prayer" about how pagan philosophers had contempt for Christians who asked God for things as opposed to praying to come into harmony with God's will (8–9).

7. See the invocation of the local gods in *Phaedrus* (261a) and the concluding prayer (279b–c); and Timaeus's invocation of the gods before his speech (*Timaeus* 27c).

8. I have borrowed this image from E. R. Dodds, "Tradition and Personal Achievement in the Philosophy of Plotinus," in *The Ancient Concept of Progress and Other Essays on Greek Literature and Belief* (Oxford: Clarendon, 1973), 126–40. See also Hadot's *Plotinus* and Andrew Louth's chapter on Plotinus in his *The Origins of the Christian Mystical Tradition: From Plato to Denys* (Oxford: Clarendon, 1981).

9. "If then there is to be conscious apprehension of the powers which are present in this way, we must turn our power of apprehension inwards, and make it attend to what is there. It is as if someone was expecting to hear a voice which he wanted to hear and withdrew from other sounds and roused his power of hearing to catch what, when it comes, is the best of all sounds which can be heard; so here we must let perceptible sounds go (except insofar as we must listen to them) and keep the soul's power of apprehension pure and ready to hear the voices from on high" (*Enneads* V.1.12).

Chapter 3: The Inward Turn

1. For translations of the *Confessions*, I use *Augustine: Confessions*, trans. F. J. Sheed (Indianapolis: Hackett, 2006). Citations include the book and section numbers from the *Confessions* and the page number from this edition. For Augustine and mysticism, see Bernard McGinn, "Augustine: The Founding Father," in *The Foundations of Mysticism: Origins to the Fifth Century* (New York: Crossroad, 1991), 228–64; as well as McGinn, "Visions and Visualization in the Here and Hereafter," *Harvard Theological Review* 98 (2005): 227–46; Denys Turner, "The God Within: Augustine's *Confessions*," in *The Darkness of God: Negativity in Christian Mysticism* (Cambridge: Cambridge University Press, 1995), 50–73; Andrew Louth, *The Origins of the Christian Mystical Tradition: From Plato to Denys* (Oxford: Clarendon, 1981), 132–58; and James J.

O'Donnell, *Augustine: Confessions*, 3 vols. (Oxford: Oxford University Press, 1992), which is also online and searchable at stoa.org/hippo.

2. See *Conf*. VII.7.

3. For this affective and relational aspect of Augustine's theology, I am indebted to Janet Soskice, "Monica's Tears: Augustine on Words and Speech," *New Blackfriars* 83 (2002): 448–58.

4. The italics represent biblical quotations.

5. "A man who makes confession to Thee does not thereby give Thee any information as to what is happening within him" (*Conf*. V.1, 75).

6. Janet Soskice makes this point in "Monica's Tears," cited in note 3 above. And compare Augustine's use of the language of infancy to Pierre Hadot's summary of elite pagan attitudes toward the body: "This age was disgusted by the body. This, moreover, was one of the reasons for pagan hostility towards the mystery of the Incarnation. As Porphyry put it clearly: 'How can we admit that the divine became an embryo, and that after its birth, it was wrapped in swaddling clothes, covered with blood, bile, and even worse things?'" (*Plotinus, or The Simplicity of Vision*, trans. Michael Chase [Chicago: University of Chicago Press, 1993], 23).

7. "Augustine was introduced to a number of 'Platonic books.' . . . They may have amounted to only a smallish portion of the *Enneads*; most of what Augustine knew of Plotinus could have been derived, or intelligently inferred, from a very few of Plotinus' earliest (and often easiest) essays: 1.6 ('On Beauty'), 5.1 ('On the Three Divine Hypostases'), 4.8 ('On the Descent of the Soul into the Body')." John M. Rist, *Augustine: Ancient Thought Baptized* (Cambridge: Cambridge University Press, 1994), 3.

8. "If I said *Trust in God*, my soul did not obey—naturally, because the [friend] whom she had loved and lost was nobler and more real than the imagined deity in whom I was bidding her trust" (*Conf*. IV.4, 60).

9. See Michael S. Sherwin, "Aquinas, Augustine, and the Medieval Scholastic Crisis concerning Charity," *On Love and Virtue: Theological Essays* (Steubenville, OH: Emmaus Academic, 2018), 67–105: "For Augustine, as well as for his Neo-Platonic sources, love's desire is ecstatic: it leads us out of ourselves toward union with God. This ecstatic enjoyment is so profound that it leads to a type of self-forgetfulness: God's plans become our plans; God's concerns, our concerns; God's will, our will. . . . We become blessed not by enjoying God 'as the soul does the body or itself, or as one friend enjoys another, but as the eye enjoys light' [citing Augustine, *City of God* VIII.8]. Augustine subsequently reveals that this depiction of enjoyment of God comes from Plotinus, who discovered that the source of both human and angelic happiness is 'a certain intelligible light' [again citing *City of God* VIII.8]. This light 'illuminates them that they may be penetrated with light and enjoy perfect happiness in the participation of God' [*City of God* X.2]" (71).

10. For Augustine's hierarchy of ways of seeing (corporal, spiritual, and intellectual), see James O'Donnell's commentary on *Confessions* VII.10.16, electronic edition available at www.stoa.org/hippo; as well as Augustine's own account in *On Genesis Literally Interpreted* XII.7.16. See also Margaret Miles, "Vision: The

Eye of the Body and the Eye of the Mind in Saint Augustine's 'De trinitate' and 'Confessions,'" *Journal of Religion* 63 (1983): 125–42; and Frederick Van Fleteren, "*Acies mentis* (Gaze of the Mind)," in *Augustine through the Ages: An Encyclopedia*, ed. Allan D. Fitzgerald (Grand Rapids: Eerdmans, 1999), 5–6.

11. Plotinus provides a similar account of how to imagine the real but intelligible world of pure light (*Enneads* V.8.9).

12. Phillip Cary, "Inward Turn and Intellectual Vision," in *Augustine's Invention of the Inner Self: The Legacy of a Christian Platonist* (New York: Oxford University Press, 2000), 63–76.

13. For this, see McGinn's section entitled "*Imago Trinitatis:* The Trinitarian Basis of Augustine's Mysticism," in *Foundations of Mysticism*, 243–48.

14. During his Platonic ascent of Book VII, Augustine had also described his soaring as an interior plunge: "Being admonished by all this to return to myself, I entered into my own depths" in order to look "with the eye of my soul" (*Conf.* VII.10, 128).

15. Analogously, Augustine, in his Platonic ascent, had said that his mind "in the thrust of a trembling glance . . . arrived at That Which Is" (*Conf.* VII.17, 133).

16. Analogously, Plotinus had said earlier, "If anyone sees it [that is, the Good], what passion will he feel, what longing in his desire to be united with it, what a shock of delight! . . . He who has seen it glories in its beauty. . . . He laughs at all other loves and despises what he thought beautiful before; it is like the experience of those who have met appearances of gods or spirits and do not any more appreciate as they did the beauty of other bodies" (*Enneads* I.6, 253).

Chapter 4: The Darkness of God

1. On the basis of the doctrine of creation ex nihilo, Christians make clear demarcations between the everlasting Father and creation; but ancient paganism, putting forward the idea of "emanation," saw all things as in continuity with the Good and thus identical with the One in their core of cores.

2. "Then certain philosophers of the Epicureans, and of the Stoics, encountered him. And some said, What will this babbler say? other some, He seemeth to be a setter forth of strange gods: because he preached unto them Jesus, and the resurrection. And they took him, and brought him unto Areopagus, saying, May we know what this new doctrine, whereof thou speakest, is? For thou bringest certain strange things to our ears: we would know therefore what these things mean. (For all the Athenians and strangers which were there spent their time in nothing else, but either to tell, or to hear some new thing.)" (Acts 17:18–21).

3. These parenthetical citations come from Pseudo-Dionysius, *Mystical Theology*, in *Pseudo-Dionysius: The Complete Works*, trans. Colm Luibheid, Classics of Western Spirituality (Mahwah, NJ: Paulist Press, 1987), 133–42.

4. Gregory Rocca, *Speaking the Incomprehensible God: Thomas Aquinas on the Interplay of Positive and Negative Theology* (Washington, DC: Catholic University of America Press, 2008), 5.

5. For a linguistic sketch of such "negative" words, see Gregory Rocca's chapter "A Brief Survey of Negative Theology in the Hellenistic and Patristic Traditions," in *Speaking the Incomprehensible God*, 3–26.

6. Rocca, *Speaking the Incomprehensible God*, 12.

7. For a panoramic introduction to Dionysius, see Andrew Louth, *Denys the Areopagite* (London: Continuum, 1989), as well as Bernard McGinn, "Anagogy and Apophaticism: The Mysticism of Dionysius," in *The Foundations of Mysticism: Origins to the Fifth Century* (New York: Crossroad, 1991), 157–82.

8. In particular, Dionysius, being a good Platonist, uses the image of light radiating out from the sun (see *Divine Names* 4). For a whole series of images of flowing, see "Ninth Letter" 1105A.

9. Pseudo-Dionysius, *The Divine Names* 4, in Luibheid, *Pseudo-Dionysius: The Complete Works*, 71–96.

10. Pseudo-Dionysius, *Divine Names* 13.2, in Luibheid, *Pseudo-Dionysius: The Complete Works*, 128.

11. Pseudo-Dionysius, *Divine Names* 4.13. Here I have used Andrew Louth's beautiful translation from *The Origins of the Christian Mystical Tradition: From Plato to Denys* (Oxford: Clarendon, 1981), 176.

12. Pseudo-Dionysius, "Ninth Letter" 1112A–B, in Luibheid, *Pseudo-Dionysius: The Complete Works*, 287.

13. Pseudo-Dionysius, *Celestial Hierarchy* 3.1, in Luibheid, *Pseudo-Dionysius: The Complete Works*, 153–54.

14. Quoted in Eric Perl, *Theophany: The Neoplatonic Philosophy of Dionysius the Areopagite*, SUNY Series in Ancient Greek Philosophy (Albany, NY: SUNY Press, 2008), 135n18.

15. Pseudo-Dionysius, "Ninth Letter" 1109C, in Luibheid, *Pseudo-Dionysius: The Complete Works*, 286.

16. On this, see Perl's chapter "Beyond Being and Intelligibility," in *Theophany*, 5–16.

17. See McGinn, *Foundations of Mysticism*, 139–42; Louth, *Origins of the Christian Mystical Tradition*, 78–94; and the introduction in Jean Daniélou, *From Glory to Glory: Texts from Gregory of Nyssa's Mystical Writings* (Crestwood, NY: St. Vladimir's Seminary Press, 1997).

18. These parenthetical citations come from Gregory of Nyssa, *The Life of Moses*, trans. Abraham J. Malherbe and Everett Ferguson, Classics of Western Spirituality (Mahwah, NJ: Paulist Press, 1980). Each citation includes the section number within *Life of Moses*, followed by the page number on which that quotation appears.

19. "And he said, I beseech thee, shew me thy glory. And he said, . . . I will be gracious, and will shew mercy on whom I will shew mercy. And he said, Thou canst not see my face: for there shall no man see me, and live. And the LORD said, Behold, there is a place by me, and thou shalt stand upon a rock: And it shall come to pass, while my glory passeth by, that I will put thee in a clift of the rock, and will cover thee with my hand while I pass by: And I will take away mine hand, and thou shalt see my back parts: but my face shall not be seen" (Exod. 33:18–23).

20. Daniélou, *From Glory to Glory*, 69.

21. Quoted in Bernard McGinn, *The Harvest of Mysticism in Medieval Germany* (New York: Crossroad, 2005), 104.

22. Quoted in McGinn, *Harvest of Mysticism*, 101.

23. Unless otherwise noted, the parenthetical citations of Eckhart quotations in the following paragraphs come from *Meister Eckhart: Selected Writings*, trans. Oliver Davies, Penguin Classics (London: Penguin, 1994).

24. Here I have used the translation found in *Meister Eckhart: The Essential Sermons, Commentaries, Treatises, and Defense*, trans. Edmund Colledge and Bernard McGinn, Classics of Western Spirituality (Mahwah, NJ: Paulist Press, 1981), 183–84.

25. "God is merry and laughs at good deeds, whereas all other works which are not done to God's glory are like ashes in God's sight" (Sermon 91, 445).

26. *The Book of Divine Consolation*, in Davies, *Meister Eckhart: Selected Writings*, 50–51.

Chapter 5: Praying with the Whole World

1. Gregory the Great, *Life of Benedict*, in *Saint Gregory the Great: Dialogues*, trans. Odo Zimmerman, Fathers of the Church 39 (Washington, DC: Catholic University of America Press, 1959), 55–56.

2. "If you are unable to cultivate stillness with ease in your regions, direct your purpose towards voluntary exile and apply your thinking to this with diligence. Be like a very good businessman, evaluating everything with regard to the cultivation of stillness and always retaining those things that are peaceful and useful in this regard. . . . Indeed, I tell you, love voluntary exile, for it separates you from the circumstances of your own country and allows you to enjoy the unique benefit of practising stillness" (*Evagrius of Pontus: The Greek Ascetic Corpus*, trans. Robert E. Sinkewicz [Oxford: Oxford University Press, 2006], 7). Unless otherwise indicated, all translations of Evagrius (except those from his *Kephalaia Gnostika*) come from Sinkewicz, even if I prefer John Bamberger's *The Praktikos and Chapters on Prayer*, Cistercian Studies 4 (Kalamazoo, MI: Cistercian Publications, 1981) as a stand-alone volume.

Below I will cite a number of Evagrian treatises. I'll give the name of the treatise, followed by the number of the "thought" (Evagrius divided his treatises into numbered lists of "quick thoughts" or maxims). One can find these treatises in the Sinkewicz edition cited above: *To Eulogios: On the Confession of Thoughts and Counsels in Their Regard* (29–59); *To Eulogios: On the Vices as Opposed to the Virtues* (60–65); *Praktikos*, entitled in Sinkewicz as *The Monk: A Treatise on the Practical Life* (91–114); *On Prayer* (183–210); and *Reflections* (210–16).

For Evagrius's fragmented and difficult advanced works, see *Evagrius's "Kephalaia Gnostika": A New Translation of the Unreformed Text from the Syriac*, trans. Ilaria L. E. Ramelli (Atlanta: SBL Press, 2015). Ramelli's overview of Evagrius is superb.

3. *The Sayings of the Desert Fathers: The Alphabetical Collection*, trans. Benedicta Ward (New York: Macmillan, 1975).

4. (Citations from *Sayings* include the page number followed by the saying number.) Compare Abba Silvanus: "The Fathers used to say that someone met Abba Silvanus one day and saw his face and body shining like an angel and he fell with his face to the ground. He said that others also had obtained this grace" (*Sayings*, 224:12). The same sort of thing would be said of Francis. See Bonaventure's *Life of St. Francis*, discussed below.

5. "Abba Poemen said, 'If the soul keeps far away from all discourse in words, from all disorder and human disturbance, the Spirit of God will come in to her and she who was barren will be fruitful'" (*Sayings*, 195:205).

6. Evagrius, *Praktikos* 72, in Bamberger, *Praktikos*, 35.

7. Augustine Casiday, *Evagrius Ponticus* (London: Routledge, 2007), 7.

8. See Bernard McGinn, *The Foundations of Mysticism: Origins to the Fifth Century* (New York: Crossroad, 1991), 144.

9. "When the mind has put off the old self and shall put on the one born of grace, . . . then it will see its own state in the time of prayer resembling sapphire or the colour of heaven" (*To Eulogios: On the Confession of Thoughts and Counsels in Their Regard*, in Sinkewicz, *Evagrius of Pontus*, 39). See also William Harmless and Raymond Fitzgerald, "The Sapphire Light of the Mind: The *Skemmata* of Evagrius Ponticus," *Theological Studies* 62 (2001): 498–529.

10. "Prayer is a communion of the mind with God. What sort of state does the mind need so that it can reach out to its Lord without turning back and commune with him without an intermediary?" (*On Prayer* 3, in Sinkewicz, *Evagrius of Pontus*, 193).

11. *On Prayer* 50, in Sinkewicz, *Evagrius of Pontus*, 198.

12. Columba Stewart, *Cassian the Monk* (New York: Oxford University Press, 1998), 43, 47.

13. For a scholarly treatment of such *theoria physike*, see Joshua Lollar's *To See into the Life of Things: The Contemplation of Nature in Maximus the Confessor and His Predecessors* (Turnhout: Brepols, 2013). For an argument for the critical importance of this ancient concept, see Bruce Foltz, *The Noetics of Nature: Environmental Philosophy and the Holy Beauty of the Visible* (New York: Fordham University Press, 2014).

14. Quoted in Donald St. John's fascinating "The Flowering of Natural Contemplation: Some Notes on *Theoria Physike* in Thomas Merton's Unpublished 'An Introduction to Christian Mysticism,'" *Merton Seasonal* 23, no. 2 (1998): 15.

15. Thomas Merton, *The Waters of Siloe* (New York: Harcourt Brace, 1949), 273–74.

16. *The Journals of Thomas Merton*, vol. 5, *Dancing in the Water of Life: Seeking Peace in the Hermitage, 1963–1965*, ed. Robert E. Daggy (New York: HarperSanFrancisco, 1997), 39–40. This is the journal in which Merton describes his move to his hermitage at Gethsemani.

17. Isaac the Syrian, *The Heart of Compassion: Daily Readings with St. Isaac of Syria*, trans. Sebastian Brock (London: Darton, Longman & Todd, 1989), 9. For Dostoyevsky's use of Isaac, see Bruce Foltz's chapter "The Glory of God Hidden in Creation: Eastern Views of Nature in Fyodor Dostoevsky and St. Isaac the Syrian," in *Noetics of Nature*, 187–202.

18. "The Great Letter," in Casiday, *Evagrius Ponticus*, 66.

19. Evagrius, *Kephalaia Gnostika* 5.39, in Ramelli, *Evagrius's "Kephalaia Gnostika,"* 279.

20. Evagrius, *Reflections* 20; *Kephalaia* 3.19; *On Prayer* 60, in Sinkewicz, *Evagrius of Pontus*, 213, 199.

21. Evagrius, *On Thoughts* 40, in Sinkewicz, *Evagrius of Pontus*, 180.

22. For a whimsical, romantic, and inspiring discussion of the growth and importance of Benedictine monasticism, see John Henry Newman's "The Mission of St. Benedict," first published in *Atlantis* in January 1858, available at http://www.newmanreader.org/works/historical/volume2/benedictine/mission .html. For a modern translation of and introduction to the *Rule*, see *RB 1980*, ed. and trans. Timothy Fry (Collegeville, MN: Liturgical Press, 1981). All citations come from this edition.

23. I analyze Hugh's little treatise *On the Three Days* below. It can be found in *Trinity and Creation: A Selection of Works of Hugh, Richard and Adam of St. Victor*, Victorine Texts in Translation 1, ed. Boyd Taylor Coolman and Dale M. Coulter (Hyde Park, NY: New City Press, 2011), 49–102. My favorite discussions of the intellectual and spiritual program of the Abbey of St. Victor are *From Knowledge to Beatitude: St. Victor, Twelfth-Century Scholars, and Beyond: Essays in Honor of Grover A. Zinn Jr.*, ed. E. Ann Matter and Lesley Smith (Notre Dame, IN: University of Notre Dame Press, 2013); and Franklin T. Harkins, *Reading and the Work of Restoration: History and Scripture in the Theology of Hugh of St. Victor* (Toronto: Pontifical Institute of Mediaeval Studies, 2009).

24. My translation of Hugh's Latin in *La "Descriptio mappe mundi" de Hugues de Saint-Victor: Texte inédit avec introduction et commentaire*, ed. Patrick Gautier Dalché (Paris: Études Augustiniennes, 1988).

25. Patrick Gautier Dalché, "Maps in Words: The Descriptive Logic of Medieval Geography, from the Eighth to the Twelfth Century," in *The Hereford World Map: Medieval World Maps and Their Context*, ed. P. D. A. Harvey (London: British Library, 2006), 231.

26. *Patrologia Latina* 176:704 (author's trans.). *De arca Noe morali*, *De arca Noe mystica* (called *Libellus de formatione arche* by its modern editor, Patrice Sicard), and *De vanitate mundi* can be found in *Patrologia Latina* 176:617–740.

27. *Patrologia Latina* 176:704 (author's trans.).

28. Author's translation.

29. I have taken this from his commentary on Dionysius's *Celestial Hierarchy* (*Patrologia Latina* 175) (author's trans.).

30. I give chapter and section numbers in my parenthetical citations.

31. See *The Soul's Journey into God*, in *Bonaventure*, trans. Ewert Cousins, Classics of Western Spirituality (Mahwah, NJ: Paulist Press, 1978), 51–116.

32. *St. Francis of Assisi: Omnibus of Sources*, ed. Marion Habig (Quincy, IL: Franciscan Press, 1991), 130–31.

33. Her *Memorial* and *Instructions* can be found in *Angela of Foligno: Complete Works*, trans. Paul Lachance, Classics of Western Spirituality (Mahwah, NJ: Paulist Press, 1993). Roman numerals refer to the chapters within the *Memorial*, followed by the page number from this edition.

34. Ariel Glucklich, *Sacred Pain: Hurting the Body for the Sake of the Soul* (Oxford: Oxford University Press, 2001), 207.

Chapter 6: How to Perform Scripture

1. "My desire now was not to be more sure of You but more steadfast in You" (*Conf.* VIII.1 [Sheed, 141]).

2. Peter of Celle, *De disciplina claustrali* (*Patrologia Latina* 202). For the translation, see "The School of the Cloister," in *Peter of Celle: Selected Works*, trans. Hugh Feiss (Kalamazoo, MI: Cistercian Publications, 1987), 73.

3. See the classic treatment of this in Jean Leclercq, *The Love of Learning and the Desire for God* (New York: Fordham University Press, 1982).

4. See Herbert Kessler, "Bright Gardens of Paradise," in *Picturing the Bible: The Earliest Christian Art*, ed. Jeffrey Spier (New Haven: Yale University Press, 2007), 111–40.

5. In addition to the references below, see Otto von Simson, "The Cistercian Contribution," in *Monasticism and the Arts*, ed. Timothy Verdon (Syracuse: Syracuse University Press, 1984), 115–38.

6. Caroline Walker Bynum, "Did the Twelfth Century Discover the Individual?," in *Jesus as Mother: Studies in the Spirituality of the High Middle Ages* (Berkeley: University of California Press, 1982), 87.

7. Quoted in R. W. Southern, "From Epic to Romance," in *The Making of the Middle Ages* (New Haven: Yale University Press, 1953), 231.

8. *Meditation* XXI (*Patrologia Latina* 158) (author's trans.). See also Southern, "From Epic to Romance," 226.

9. Bynum, "Did the Twelfth Century Discover the Individual?," 87. For overviews of broad social changes, see Southern, "From Epic to Romance," 219–57; Rachel Fulton, *From Judgment to Passion: Devotion to Christ and the Virgin Mary, 800–1200* (New York: Columbia University Press, 2002); and Sarah McNamer, *Affective Meditation and the Invention of Medieval Compassion* (Philadelphia: University of Pennsylvania Press, 2010).

10. Duncan Robertson, *Lectio Divina: The Medieval Experience of Reading* (Collegeville, MN: Liturgical Press, 2011), 134.

11. "The secret thoughts of the heart" is a paraphrase of *Cogitatio cordis mei.*

12. Bernard McGinn, *The Growth of Mysticism* (New York: Crossroad, 1994), 357–63.

13. Guigo the Carthusian, *Scala Claustralium* (*Patrologia Latina* 184); in English as *The Ladder of Monks and Twelve Meditations: A Letter on the Contemplative Life.*

14. Hugh of Balma, *The Roads to Zion Mourn*, in *Carthusian Spirituality: The Writings of Hugh of Balma and Guigo de Ponte*, trans. Dennis Martin, Classics of Western Spirituality (Mahwah, NJ: Paulist Press, 1997), 67–170.

15. As we have seen, Duncan Robertson calls *lectio divina* a "movement of reading into prayer" (*Lectio Divina*, 134).

16. "It is not presumptuous to aspire to the kiss of the mouth if one has first gained practice in the kiss of the feet and hand" (*Zion* III.1, 106).

17. Bernard McGinn, *The Harvest of Mysticism in Medieval Germany* (New York: Crossroad, 2005), 112.

18. Meister Eckhart, Sermon 12, in *Meister Eckhart: Sermons and Treatises*, trans. M. O'C. Walshe (London: Element, 1987).

19. Quoted in McGinn, *Harvest of Mysticism*, 114.

Conclusion

1. "Natural Religion teaches, it is true, the infinite power and majesty, the wisdom and goodness, the presence, the moral governance, and, in one sense, the unity of the Deity; but it gives little or no information respecting what may be called His *Personality*." John Henry Newman, "Natural and Revealed Religion," in *Fifteen Sermons Preached before the University of Oxford*, ed. James David Earnest and Gerard Tracey (Oxford: Oxford University Press, 2006), 27–28.

2. "The Christian's God does not consist merely of a God who is the author of mathematical truths and the order of the elements. That is the portion of the heathen and Epicureans. He does not consist merely of a God who extends his providence over the life and property of men so as to grant a happy span of years to those who worship him. . . . But the God of Abraham, the God of Isaac, the God of Jacob, the God of the Christians is a God of love and consolation: he is a God who fills the soul and heart of those whom he possesses." Blaise Pascal, *Pensées*, trans. A. J. Krailsheimer (London: Penguin, 1996), 169.

3. See the special issue of *Modern Theology* entitled "Creation 'ex nihilo' and Modern Theology," guest edited by Janet Soskice (29, no. 2 [2013]).

4. See Janet Martin Soskice, "Monica's Tears: Augustine on Words and Speech," *New Blackfriars* 83 (2002): 448–58; and Soskice, *The Kindness of God: Metaphor, Gender, and Religious Language* (Oxford: Oxford University Press, 2007).

5. Jean-Luc Marion, *God without Being*, trans. Thomas A. Carlson, 2nd ed. (Chicago: University of Chicago Press, 2012).

6. Falque says that if, for Marion, Mark Rothko is the painter who best exemplifies this understanding of the icon, for him it is Lucian Freud, who creates portraits of vivid presence. Emmanuel Falque, *The Wedding Feast of the Lamb: Eros, the Body, and the Eucharist*, trans. George Hughes (New York: Fordham University Press, 2016).

7. "The mystical approach of which we have been speaking must teach us in the concrete to maintain a constant closeness to *this* God; to say 'thou' to him, to commit ourselves to his silence and darkness, not be anxious lest we may lose him by the fact of calling him by a name . . . because he does not constitute one element among others in our scheme of things. It must teach us that he does not belong to any specific place in our scheme of things." Karl Rahner, "The Christian Living Formerly and Today," in *Theological Investigations*, trans. David Bourke (New York: Seabury, 1971), 16.

8. *Julian of Norwich: Showings*, trans. Edmund Colledge and James Walsh, Classics of Western Spirituality (Mahwah, NJ: Paulist Press, 1978).

9. *John Ruusbroec: The Spiritual Espousals and Other Works*, trans. James Wiseman, Classics of Western Spirituality (Mahwah, NJ: Paulist Press, 1985), 155–86.

10. For a reading of Cusanus as being between the Middle Ages and modernity, see Johannes Hoff, *The Analogical Turn: Rethinking Modernity with Nicholas of Cusa* (Grand Rapids: Eerdmans, 2013); and Thomas Pfau, "'Seeing and Being Seen Coincide': Freedom as Contemplation in Nicholas of Cusa and G. M. Hopkins," *Logos: A Journal of Catholic Thought and Culture* 22, no. 4 (2019): 20–41.

11. *On Seeking God*, in *Nicholas of Cusa: Selected Spiritual Writings*, trans. H. Lawrence Bond, Classics of Western Spirituality (Mahwah, NJ: Paulist Press, 1997), 215–32.

Index